DATE DUE

WITHDRAWN

DEMCO 38-296

GARDEN LEGACY

The Residential Landscapes of Design Workshop

Sarah Chase Shaw

Photography by D.A. Horchner

Copyright © 2010 Design Workshop, Inc.

1390 Lawrence Street, Suite 200

Denver, Colorado 80204-2048

303-623-5186

www.designworkshop.com

Published by Design Workshop, Inc.

All rights reserved. No part of this publication

may be reproduced without the express

permission of Design Workshop, Inc.

ISBN: 978-0-9827494-0-1

Printed in Canada

GARDEN LEGACY

The residential landscapes of Design Workshop and the principles that guide
an emerging philosophy about gardens in the 21st Century.

CONTENTS

FOREWORD

For over forty years, Design Workshop has practiced landscape architecture in the American West. A specific design vocabulary has evolved out of our work that is related to a geography which resonates deeply within us. Our work is identifiable because we interact with the landscape, taking our contextual cues from the climate, physiographic features, textures, patterns, and raw materials of the landscape. Our work reflects our mantra of believing in the power of place. We believe that specific knowledge of a site, such as its settlement patterns, plant communities, and regional values, are the foundation of great design. The end result makes a significant contribution to establishing a unique design character—otherwise known as regionalism.

The regional setting for the gardens represented in this book is the mountains of the American West, from Wyoming's Teton Range in the north to Arizona's Catalina Mountains in the south. The individuals and families whose gardens are highlighted within these pages have been a delight to work with because the ideas displayed are theirs. For each garden, we experienced a partnership in design that was creative, thoughtful, and truly indicative of the ways in which people experience the Western landscape. The residents of these landscapes were changed by being a part of a design process that was much larger than themselves—and they loved every aspect of it. Our role as landscape architects was to guide the development of the garden. We asked questions such as: How will the garden be used? What is the indoor-outdoor relationship? Where will the family gather for private meals? Where do outdoor recreational space and entertainment areas overlap? How will the views be contained or framed? What are the fundamental design ideas that link these spaces together?

Within these gardens, we explored the concepts of prospect (opportunity) and refuge (safety), recurring themes in dramatic and exposed landscapes. At Teton Overlook, a private and protected garden space yields to a grand vista of the Teton Range. At Capitol Valley Ranch, the enclosed north-facing entry courtyard allows only a glimpse of the surrounding landscape; the big view is revealed on the sunny south side, where it opens up to pastureland and mountains. Catalina Foothills relies on the "borrowed" landscape of distant views and the colors and patterns of native plants to position the garden in its place of origin. Aspen Terrace Garden combines the concepts of prospect and refuge in outdoor living rooms, in which a fireplace and comfortable furnishings have the ability to generate an intimate experience within the larger landscape.

The extraordinary gardens portrayed in this book are drawn from a design philosophy that combines the iconic or pictorial with a focus on a landscape character drawn from the site itself. The narrative capacity of the landscape is present in all of these gardens, represented in the spatial relationships between elements in each composition, the arrangement of plant materials, water in its varying forms, the interplay of landscape and architecture, and the ability to manage—and celebrate—the magnificent surrounding natural environment.

— Richard W. Shaw, FASLA, Principal, Design Workshop

Encountering the Land:
A 21st century Country Place era emerges in the Rocky Mountain Region

— *Charles A. Birnbaum, FASLA, FAAR*

As author Sarah Chase Shaw and photographer D.A. Horchner powerfully illustrate in *Garden Legacy*, the planning and design approach to residential landscape design in the American West, employed and carefully refined by Design Workshop over the past several decades, embodies a philosophy that "combines the iconic or pictorial with a focus on landscape character drawn from the site itself."[1] The firm has introduced a design vocabulary that until now, rather surprisingly, had been largely unrealized in residential work in the Rocky Mountain region: the Country Place estate. As illustrated in *Garden Legacy*, the design ethos of that late 19th and early 20th century period of landscape architecture has been masterfully and eloquently interpreted through a contemporary lens.

To appreciate the extent of the firm's accomplishments, we need only peruse Horchner's evocative images of the Star Mesa Ranch, the Snake River Residence, and the Aspen Terrace Garden and the supporting imagery and text in the Design Principles sections dedicated to Horizon and Framed View. In all cases, these new gardens harness and celebrate their larger scenic and ecological values. Their spatial organization and material selections, for both living elements such as plants and nonliving elements such as stone, are inspired by their larger setting: the cultural landscape of the Rocky Mountains.

To provide a historical context for the nine extraordinary contemporary gardens in this book, it is worth looking back to the Country Place era in garden and estate design that began in the 1880s and concluded with the stock market crash of 1929. During these seminal decades, grand residential properties were designed with an obvious, sometimes ostentatious, expression of affluence. One of the

greatest examples is the 125,000-acre Biltmore estate outside Asheville, North Carolina, designed by Frederick Law Olmsted beginning in 1888 and finished by his sons and Warren Manning in 1893. Their characteristic design often included formal garden styles and such features as allées, terraces, fountains, and garden sculpture. Then, as now with the gardens in this volume, the design team of architects, landscape architects, and sculptors worked in close partnership with their clients. In that earlier era, however, the goal often was to create innovative and at times extravagant gardens inspired by European and Asian precedents, which would lend a sense of tradition, age, and affluence to what, in many cases, was "new money."

These earlier designs often sought their inspiration from European Beaux-Arts design styles, resulting in a return to symmetry and more formal geometries. Prominent designers included architects Charles Platt, Guy Lowell, and Carrère and Hastings, as well as landscape architects Jens Jensen, Frederick Law Olmsted, Ellen Shipman, A. E. Hansen, and Warren Manning, to name a few.

An examination of the best known and most celebrated publications of this era, such as *American Gardens*, edited by Guy Lowell (1902) and *Beautiful Gardens in America* by Louise Shelton (1915, 1924, 1928) reveals a startling gap, and raises a question: What about the great westward expansion?

A review of Lowell's handsomely produced gilded volume reveals 46 gardens, all of which can be found east of the Mississippi, in New York, Pennsylvania, Massachusetts, New Hampshire, Maryland, Connecticut, New Jersey, Delaware, and Virginia, with "glimpses" of two South Carolina gardens. In Shelton's last revised edition of her enormously popular book, replete with hundreds of full-page black and white photographs, her national survey spans north to south along the East Coast, with additional chapters dedicated to "Illinois and Ohio, Michigan and Wisconsin, California, Washington, and Alaska and British Columbia."

Setting aside work done in California, are we to assume that nothing is happening by 1928 in Planting Zones 3 and 4, the Rocky Mountains of the American West?

To answer this question, let's consult Mac Griswold and Eleanor Weller's *The Golden Age of American Gardens: Proud Owners, Private Estates 1890-1940*, first published in 1991. The Table of Contents says it all, with the Northeast referred to as "The Powerhouse," and additional chapters dedicated to the Middle Atlantic, the South, the Deep South, the West Coast and Hawaii, and the Midwest and beyond. In fact, in the entirety of this 400-page book, the Rocky Mountain region is addressed in just three paragraphs in a subchapter, "Desert and Mountain", with only five associated images.[2] This is not a criticism of the book, but may truly be an accurate depiction of the Country Place movement, or the lack thereof, in the region.

Within the "Desert and Mountain" subchapter, one notable estate landscape embraces the unique power of place: Spencer Penrose's "El Pomar" in Colorado Springs (Figure 1). The image of a sunken garden designed by the Olmsted firm recalls The Secret Garden at Villa Gamberaia in Settignano, Italy, where the monumental scenery provided by the setting is "borrowed" by its talented designers. In fact, between 1908 and 1937, eight estate consultations in Colorado by the Olmsted firm can be documented, though five never result in the generation of any landscape plans. Of the remaining three, all are in Colorado Springs.[3] "El Pomar" was the most extensive commission; 57 drawings were generated between 1916 and 1928, with additional correspondence in 1937.

This is a surprising void when we consider the length, breadth, and diversity of all three Olmsteds in the planning and design for Denver's city and mountain parks, which spanned from 1888 to 1914. Why did the opportunity and prospects afforded during this 26-year consultation not spill over into estate and subdivision commissions, as they had in places like Louisville, Kentucky, Buffalo, New York, and Atlanta, Georgia?[4]

In her recent book, *A Genius for Place: American Landscapes of the Country Place Era* (2007), author Robin Karson celebrates an emerging American Style for estate landscapes. This publication also passes over the Rocky Mountain region, with the nearest examples from California (Lockwood de Forest's design for Val Verde) and Michigan (Jens Jensen's design for the Edsel and Eleanor Ford estate). However, its articulation of a unique style in which "wild gardens and parklike meadows were intended to provide clients with restorative experiences"[5] shares design and planning aspirations similar to the work being undertaken today by Design Workshop.

As a result of *Garden Legacy*, future garden surveys no longer will be able to leap over Zones 3 and 4 and the Rocky Mountains, but instead will linger to explore the significant work being designed and built in the intermountain West.

Figure 1: Borrowed Scenery at "El Pomar," Colorado Springs, CO (Courtesy of the Archives of American Gardens, Smithsonian Institution).

Two important ideas emerge in a discussion of this earlier estate work and what distinguishes the unique regional landscape legacy of ranches and residences designed by Design Workshop.

First, all nine gardens in this volume include a large-scale context map that places the house and garden in its larger geographic landscape of vistas and vast viewsheds, mountain ranges and topographic elevation changes, woodlands and forest, fields and meadows, streams and irrigation swales. Though the approach of embracing the larger cultural landscape may seem like a simple idea, it was not the norm in earlier regional garden surveys in the United States and abroad. For example, *Historic Gardens of Virginia* (1923) published by the James River Garden Club, *Portraits of Philadelphia Gardens* by Louise and James Bush-Brown (1929), and *Charleston Gardens* by Loutrell Briggs (1951) included the gardens constructed immediately surrounding the house and omitted the context of the larger scenic and natural setting. This same approach was taken with *Italian Villas and Gardens of the Renaissance* (1925) by John Shepherd and Geoffrey Jellicoe, whose evocative plans and axonometric drawings are of the villa landscapes only and not their larger surrounds.

Finally, this volume presents the firm's approach to planting design and the plant palette, which is unique to their work and the region. To this end, it is worth going back over a half-century to the popular handbook, *Rocky Mountain Horticulture is Different*, (1951) by George W. Kelly (Figure 2). Kelly bemoans that "we now have hundreds of books and dozens of magazines written on the various phases of horticulture. [Yet] because almost all of the horticultural literature has been written for older, more thickly populated parts of the United States, very little of it applies to the peculiar conditions found in the Rocky Mountain and Great Plains States."[6]

More than 125 years have passed since the Country Place era began, and nearly 60 years have elapsed since Kelly's call for greater reference resources for planting in Zones 3 and 4. In its design work in the Intermountain West, Design Workshop has advanced this discussion and has leapt over the garden wall to embrace the larger cultural landscape of the region.

—*Charles A. Birnbaum, FASLA, FAAR, is the Founder and President of The Cultural Landscape Foundation in Washington, D.C.*

Figure 2: Book Cover for *Rocky Mountain Horticulture is Different* (1951). Here the author, George W. Kelly opens the garden gate to the region's mountainous surrounds.

LEGACY GARDENS

The private landscapes contained within these pages were designed to foster a reverence for the land, to cultivate the creative spirit, and to inspire a principled exploration of a vast and varied geographic setting.

STAR MESA RETREAT

Like a Himalayan landscape, Star Mesa Retreat evokes a feeling of being on the roof of the world. Mountains, visible on all sides, appear on the edge of the high-meadow landscape, creating an environment of reflection and unity with the sky.

Extending the horizon with water and sky

Star Mesa Retreat, like the Himalayan landscapes explored by its owners, evokes a feeling of being on the roof of the world. A false horizon of open grassland rises from the center of this high-altitude site in Colorado's Pitkin County, giving way to mountains, visible from all sides and appearing closer than they really are. To the south, darkly forested mountainsides and snow-capped peaks tip the horizon line. To the north, arid earthen-red hillsides form an immediate contrasting backdrop to the elegantly rustic log home designed by Backen Gillam Architects of Sausalito and St. Helena, California. The sense of being at the top of the world and the solace of the natural setting present a perfect template for creating an environment that provides a setting for entertainment and recreation as well as a refuge for privacy and meditation.

Once part of a larger ranch, the property is characterized by open grasslands and punctuated by stands of native Gambel oak. The site plan and design grew out of the owners' desire to create a high-mountain environment complete with rushing water and lush woodlands, a challenge to carry out on semi-arid former pastureland. The natural slope of the property, combined with generous water rights, provided a perfect opportunity to develop an artfully asymmetrical landscape framed by the horizon. The land was gently sculpted to enhance the natural slopes of the property on a scale equal to the views; from any point, the perspective is composed and balanced. Rock outcroppings, sacred Tibetan religious objects, and beds of colorful perennials, as well as the home, are cradled in the gently sloping convex and concave curves of the landscape.

Spiritual references such as this Buddhist stupa grace open meadows and intimate garden areas, connecting the mountains and people of the Himalayas with those in Colorado.

The entertainment terrace extends to the stream. Low stone walls create edges between formal and informal living spaces. Glimpses of the pond and mountains beyond are seen through the canopy of aspen trees.

The stream exits the pond through a meadow of daylilies (*Hemerocallis* sp.), shown here in their fall color. Large boulders, stacked one on another, bolster the banks and create opportunities for stream crossings and simple lounging.

The driveway enters the property through a rustic wooden gate supported by stone pillars. Edged by native and cultivated grasses and a line of cottonwood trees, the narrow lane weaves between subtle land forms and tree massings, until the home comes into view. The land slopes away, revealing open pastures, the rugged hillside beyond, and the Woody Creek valley below. The design team developed precise topographic models of the gently rolling site to accommodate an elevation drop of forty-five feet from the property's entrance to its northern boundary.

Like many agricultural properties in the American West, the site featured an irrigation ditch, which the design team transformed into a meandering mountain stream. Emerging from a source pool at the high point of the property, the stream parallels the entry drive. It follows the property's natural elevation changes, flowing quietly through pools that mirror the sky and then suddenly surging boisterously through rocky outcrops and over steep drops anchored by granite boulders. Passing under the driveway, the water weaves in and out of manicured lawns and native-grass pastures, providing natural energy to power a series of Tibetan prayer wheels located on the stream banks. Finally emerging from the hillside through an elaborate granite waterfall, the stream flows into a large pond in front of the home.

At the point where the stream empties into the pond, the naturalized and domestic landscapes come together. The water is brought to a reflective stillness. Dense plantings of irises, willows, and daylilies converge at the outlet, slowing the water's release and obscuring the edge where land and water meet. A setting that was once open to the elements becomes an intimate place to pause and appreciate the abundance of water and the lush south-facing entertainment lawn that envelop the home. Stone terraces with low walls and deep roof overhangs bolstered by wooden posts give structure to the home's outdoor spaces, while islands of daisies, black-eyed Susans, and coneflowers add bright color and texture to the expanse of rolling green meadow and lawn. The view from the home to the horizon is controlled by undulations in the land and deliberately positioned plantings of aspen, cottonwood, and spruce trees.

The main entrance is located on the north side. Shrouded in a grove of mature aspen and spruce trees, the arrival area is reminiscent of a quiet mountain retreat: a low porte-cochère supported by log beams leads to the characteristically rustic front entrance, a door inlaid with hardware and animal carvings. Boulders covered in green lichen and a carpet of soft shade-loving groundcovers suggest deep, dark, and protected forest land, in contrast with the open vistas and arid landscapes found on the south side of the house.

Slightly removed from the home, the swimming pool and spa perch on the edge of a steep hillside, facing east and overlooking the Woody Creek Valley. Subtle topographic sculpting renders the pool and spa visually accessible but physically removed from the main entertainment area. Viewed from above, the water surface merges with the valley beyond in an infinite edge, suggesting that the water simply disappears into the abyss below. A sandstone patio follows the curvi-linear outline of the pool and spa, fracturing into smaller pieces as it disappears into the surrounding lawn. Masses of vivid magenta-flowering sedum and soft white daisies offer color and foreground perspective in this retreat's views to the east.

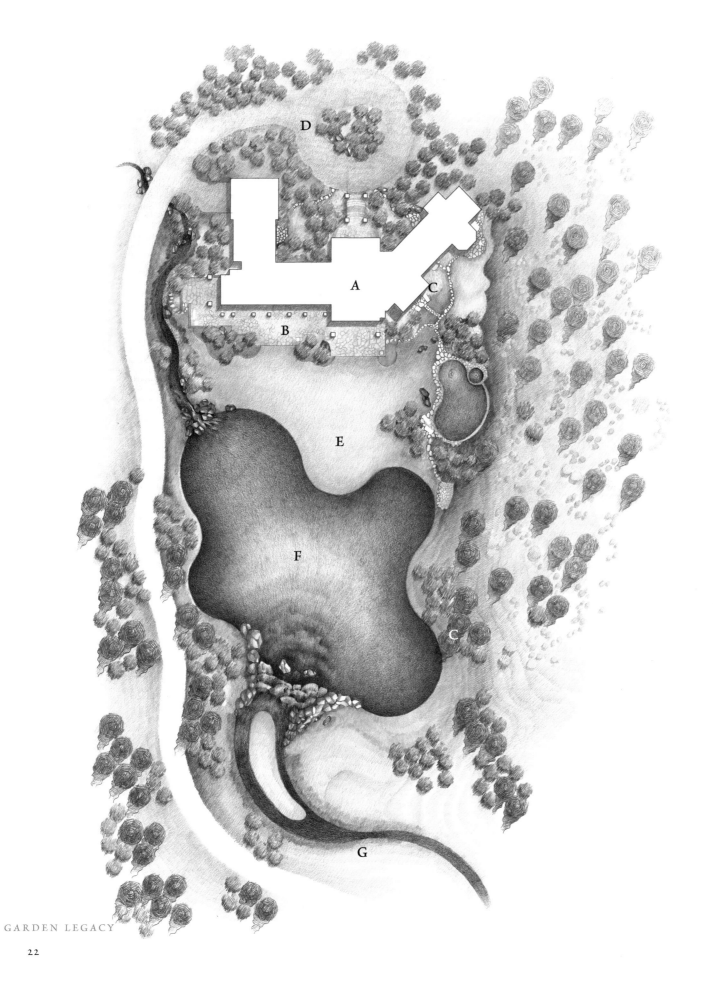

A. Residence

B. Patio

C. Perennial Garden

D. Auto Court

E. Lawn

F. Pond

G. Meadow

0' 10' 20'   40'

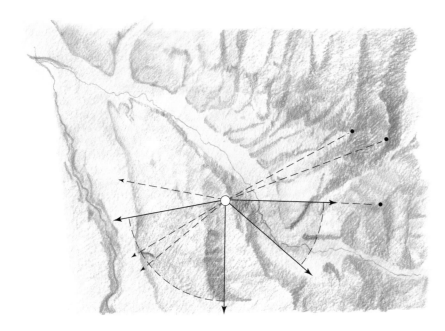

(Above) Views to the south from this garden include grassy pasturelands that slope upward to a point where they appear to join the sky at the horizon. Visible on this line are the peaks of surrounding mountains. To the north, the land drops off to reveal an agricultural valley below and rust-colored hillsides beyond.

(Right) Topographic drops in the stream course are accommodated by subtle grading and the placement of boulders and river cobble. The rush of water at these points add movement and vibrancy to the landscape.

STAR MESA RETREAT

23

The vivid late-summer blooms of purple coneflower
(*Echinacea purpurea*) and black-eyed Susan (*Rudebeckia* sp.)
lining the entry drive appear even more intensely colorful
in the high-mountain sunlight.

(*Opposite*) The infinity-edge swimming pool and spa perch on the precipice of a steep hillside overlooking the Woody Creek Valley. Subtle sculpting of the land adds topographic interest and provides a sheltering space for the curvilinear pool and spa. Surrounding them, a patio of Colorado sandstone "disappears" into the lawn as it moves away from the water. A stand of aspen trees frames the view eastward to the mountains.

(*Above*) The abstract shape of the pool is echoed in the sculpted masses of magenta-flowering sedum (*Sedum spurium* 'Dragon's Blood') and daisies (*Chrysanthemum leucanthemum*).

Carved out of the surrounding landscape, the pond
introduces a human scale to the vast landscape. Reflections
in the water's surface unite the landscape with the sky
and the distant view to the mountains.

SNAKE RIVER RESIDENCE

A slice of Modernism in a rustic environment, Snake River Residence challenges the notions of contemporary design in a rugged landscape. Respect for the natural riparian landscape is evident in the use of native materials and the restoration of the site's natural systems. Trees, shrubs, and perennials are placed in grid patterns, formalizing the organization of these natural elements in a distinctive and thoughtful manner.

The east-facing terrace is broad and accommodating, with low seating walls creating an edge and containing the space. Small river cobble set on its side marks the center of the terrace with a rectilinear outline, providing a contrast with the sandstone paving. The meadow was created by carefully thinning existing cottonwood saplings to suggest a drier and broader environment reminiscent of an open mountain meadow.

Weaving contemporary outdoor living spaces into a restored riparian environment

Set amid a mature riparian cottonwood bosque near Wyoming's Snake River, just outside of Grand Teton National Park, Snake River Residence is part of a community of homes discretely nestled along Fish Creek and its meandering small tributaries. Designed by the late architect William F. Tull, the contemporary single-story stone and stucco home and guest house allowed for the creation of a variety of outdoor spaces in courtyards and alcoves created by the highly articulated exterior walls. The landscape architect took advantage of all the angles and intersections of materials to design interesting and usable outdoor spaces around the perimeter of the house. Climate conditions, including wind, snow, and great fluctuations of heat and cold, encouraged the creation of microclimates in which native plants and water are combined with bold geometric lines. The resulting design weaves a modern aesthetic of color, texture, and focus into the surrounding natural environment.

The design team created a site plan for the main house, which is shaped like an elongated cross, with four distinct outdoor spaces and varying points of reference. Oriented toward the mountains, the driveway emerges from the forest into a field of glacial erratics surrounding the auto court. These monolithic stones jutting out of the landscape like miniature mountain ranges suggest the region's geologic upheaval and exposure to often-extreme weather. Placed sequentially from small to large, they emerge from the level ground to form a passageway into

Accented by glacial erratics, a sinuous stream of aggregate riverstone, and a forest of columnar aspen trees, the auto court offers a literal translation of the nearby Snake River corridor. Boulders are placed upright, overlapping one another in a manner that echoes the Teton Range to the north.

the sandstone courtyard. A band of aggregate river rock snakes across the hard surface of the auto court.

From the living room, the view to the north changes seasonally. In winter, the Grand Teton and adjacent peaks rise dramatically over the tops of the trees lining the river bottom. In the summer, a dense canopy of leaves all but masks the mountains in the distance, and the scene becomes more intimate and secluded. In the foreground, a meadow of native grasses and wildflowers extends outward, connecting the residence to the mountains, forest, and river landscape. A stone path winds in and out of the meadow, pausing at carefully placed hand-hewn benches and places with views of sculpture in the foreground and the Grand Teton in the distance.

On the east side, the spa is tucked into a courtyard that separates the master bedroom suite from the rest of the house. Protected from the elements, the spa and outdoor fireplace are all but indiscernible from the exterior of the house. Square sandstone steps lead away from the spa, paralleling a runnel of water bordered by native grasses. Extending from the east facade, a raised boardwalk crosses a reclaimed spring creek to provide access to Fish Creek, a tributary of the Snake River. Edged in native Rocky Mountain iris, the boardwalk connects the main house to an observation point in the distance, minimizing human activity in the wetlands area. During construction, much attention was given to restoring the ecological integrity of the riparian areas, which had become degraded during the property's former use as a cattle ranch. Native grasses, sedges, reeds, and cattails were reintroduced to contain the soil erosion and upgrade the water quality.

On the sunny south side of the home, next to the great room, a generously sized sandstone terrace designed for outdoor entertaining and dining looks out onto riparian meadows. Inlaid with bands of tiny river cobble and edged by low seating walls, the terrace extends to intersect, almost imperceptibly, with the untamed environment of the native river bottom. A reflecting pool extends south more than one hundred feet from the great room terrace. Shallow and still, the water reflects a large totem sculpture at the far end of the pool and the canopy of trees and open sky overhead, integrating the larger landscape into the living area next to the home. A formal grid of aspen trees separates the pool from the outdoor dining area. An understory of brilliant Johnson's Blue geranium fills the ground west of the pool. Flanking the east side, long lines of blue oat grass separate the native meadow from the pool's edge.

Trees, planted at entryways and at intersecting planes of the architecture, rise above the low residence, softening its profile on the forest floor. At an elevation of over six thousand feet, with windy conditions and wide fluctuations in temperature, plant choices are extremely limited. The landscape architects experimented with cottonwood and aspen trees, staples of the surrounding environment, planting them in formal grid patterns, an arrangement more commonly used with street trees in urban environments. The tight and columnar effect of this planting style merges the unprogrammed nature of the surrounding environment with the modern and more geometric aesthetic of the home.

The reflecting pool appears to drop magically off the terrace into the cottonwood forest. Flanking the pool, planting areas are organized to complement the native landscape. The use of indigenous meadow plants such as little bluestem (*Schizachyrium scoparium*), combined with native trees and shrubs, helps the designed landscape blend seamlessly with the existing natural place.

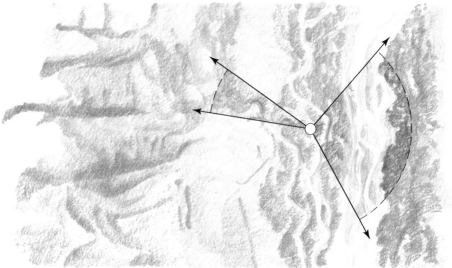

(*Above*) Enclosed in a dense cottonwood bosque along a tributary of the Snake River, the home and garden nestle into the landscape, translating the riparian environment into a formal landscape that celebrates the surrounding natural setting.

(*Left*) A sandstone path parallels a water channel leading away from the spa courtyard next to the house. Representative of the spring creeks along the Snake River, the runnel is bordered by blue fescue (*Festuca glauca*) and tufted hair grass (*Deschampsia cespitosa*), transitioning to native Rocky Mountain iris (*Iris missouriensis*) and the wetlands environment.

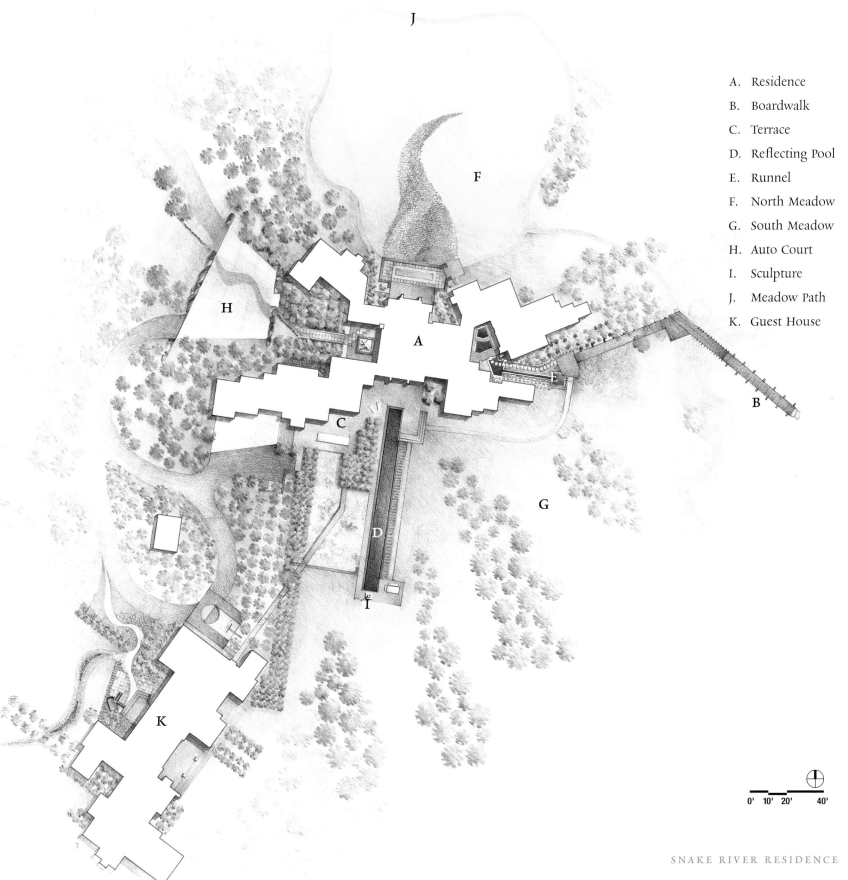

A. Residence

B. Boardwalk

C. Terrace

D. Reflecting Pool

E. Runnel

F. North Meadow

G. South Meadow

H. Auto Court

I. Sculpture

J. Meadow Path

K. Guest House

J

F

H

A

C

E

B

D

G

I

K

0' 10' 20'   40'

SNAKE RIVER RESIDENCE

37

(Above) A stone path meanders through the meadow on the north side of the house. Clumps of native lupine (*Lupinus* sp.) grow intermittently, adding midsummer color to the cottonwood forest.

(Opposite) The designers gave special attention to improving the habitat along the spring creeks throughout the property. Intensive grazing had compromised the wetlands, and the design team used a systems approach to restore the ecosystems, water quality, and vegetation on the site.

The pool's glassy surface reflects the home's architectural qualities, as well as the changing colors and patterns of the sky and seasons. Aspens, planted in a formal grid, parallel the pool, providing shelter and sculptural beauty against the modern lines of the house.

WOODY CREEK GARDEN

Within walled boundaries, the Woody Creek Garden embraces a hillside, offering a contemporary Arts and Crafts interpretation of a rooftop terrace with long views to the valley below and mountains beyond. Water is the unifying element: atmospheric mist, still pools, singly focused rivulets, and cascading thin mirrors create an environment of privacy and mystery linked to the surrounding high-mountain forests.

Celebrating water in its infinite forms

Located on a steep hillside overlooking the Roaring Fork River Valley in Colorado, the Woody Creek Garden is an assemblage of outdoor living environments wrapped around a home atop high stone walls that separate development from the carefully protected landscape. A strong mountain-garden vocabulary is established through the use of water, expressed in multiple artistic ways, and native plants, whose ability to thrive at an altitude of over seven thousand feet is enhanced by the creation of walled microclimates.

The owners of the Arts and Crafts-style shingle home, designed by Poss Architecture + Planning in Aspen, and the design team agreed that preserving the environmental characteristics and significant topographic nature of the site was essential. Instead of damaging a large swath of hillside with a sprawling floor plan, the team designed the home and gardens together with a smaller footprint, using the slope to stack uses beneath the main living spaces and a wraparound rooftop terrace that is accessed by and visible from all areas of the U-shaped structure. A principal component of the design is the seamless visual interplay between exterior and interior spaces; the terrace and natural landscape beyond are visible from every room in the house.

During construction, the steep and forested hillside environment remained virtually untouched. Layered architectural elements allowed for the garden to be carefully, almost surgically, placed within the walled preserve. On the south side, high walls separate the terrace gardens and the natural landscape and extend the living environment to a promontory overlooking the valley.

(Above) A runnel carved into the stone cap funnels a rivulet of water toward Mt. Sopris in the distance. This glimpse to the west is the only opening in the tightly enclosed entry courtyard.

(Opposite) The entry courtyard is ringed by a column of aspen trees. Granite-slab benches are placed within the space for gathering and quiet contemplation. Water bubbles out of a granite cube, creating a visual and audible centerpiece in the space. The trickle echoes off the tightly hewn stone of the garden walls and building façade.

The existing site conditions—including thick stands of aspen trees, wildflower meadows, and views worthy of a Maxfield Parrish painting—played an important role in the design for the property and the use of native plants and water to create an environment that blends with the landscape.

Water is an essential theme and defining element of form in the design of the garden spaces. A series of illusionary design ideas explores various manifestations of water. Still water reflects elements in the sky that are hidden to the naked eye. Planes of water fracture and fall, melting in a curtain-like formation behind a spa. A rivulet of water funneled through a strategically placed gap in a wall flows toward a distant Mt. Sopris vista. A granite cube overflows with water, the sound of the spray echoing vibrantly in an enclosed stone courtyard. Mist softly blankets the courtyard, creating the sensation of being enveloped in a cloud. Everywhere in the garden, water helps define designed spaces, mirroring and serving as a constant reminder of the power of the sun and clouds, the mutable character of the sky, and the atmospheric changes that animate this high mountain landscape.

Within the north-facing entrance courtyard, the vapor from the granite-fountain centerpiece generates an atmosphere of ethereal mystery. A carpet of creeping potentilla softens the base of the fountain, repeating the colors of the aspen canopy that encloses the entire space like a lid. Linear slabs of granite surround the fountain. The crisp white columns of the aspens' trunks contrast with the dark surfaces and hard edges of the granite. To the side of the entry gate, a small rectilinear cut in the stone wall frames a view to the west, creating a singular reference to the outside world in this encased space. A miniscule fountain

bubbles in the center of the opening. The water is carried away in a narrow runnel, disappearing into the framed horizon.

On the south side of the home lies the entertainment lawn. In contrast to the enclosed and private nature of the entry courtyard, this grand space opens to the expansive natural landscape above and below. A square of lawn doubles as a green roof over the service area. A rectilinear pool, rimmed in honed black granite, reflects the changing natural environment on its taut surface. The shallow water disappears over the infinity edge, cascading into a pool located below the wall. A curved metal sculpture appears to float in the pool, framing views within its arc. A wall of water in a corner adds an element of surprise to the horizontal plane. Water appears to melt out of a retaining wall, forming a thin and reflective vertical surface. A rectilinear pool lies behind the wall, silently mirroring the sky above and offering no ostensible connection to the structure or to its source. Sandstone terraces embrace the house, extending toward the views. A stone stairway breaks through the terrace wall, leading down to a patio with a fire pit in a gathering area that joins at grade the designed and natural environments.

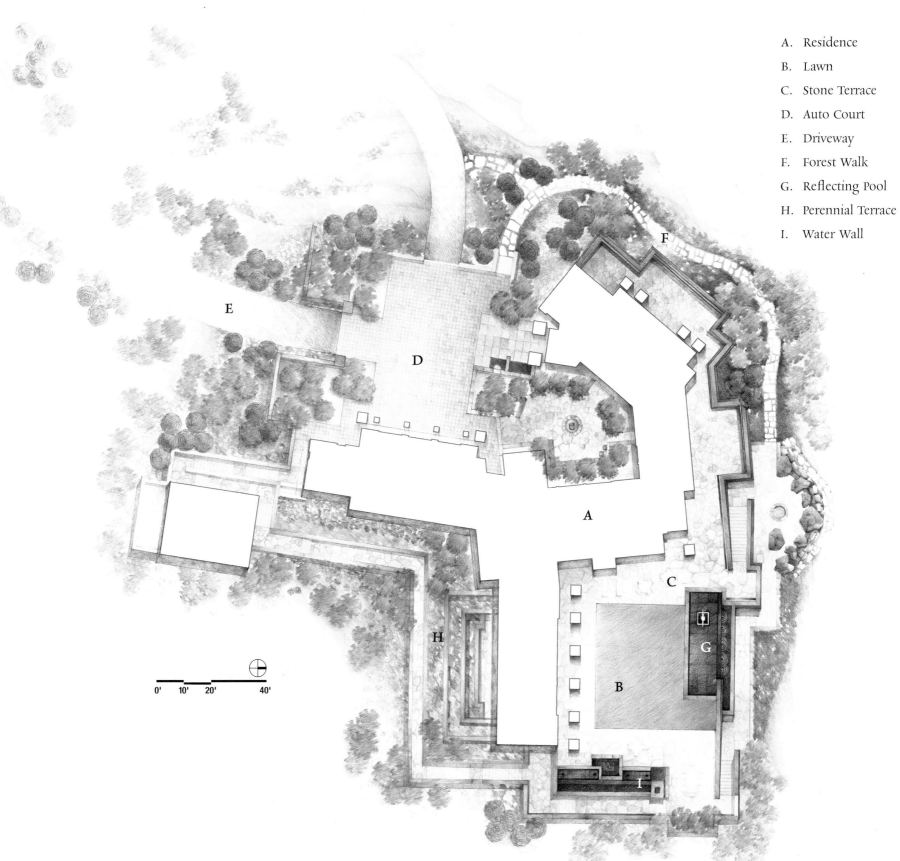

A. Residence
B. Lawn
C. Stone Terrace
D. Auto Court
E. Driveway
F. Forest Walk
G. Reflecting Pool
H. Perennial Terrace
I. Water Wall

0' 10' 20'   40'

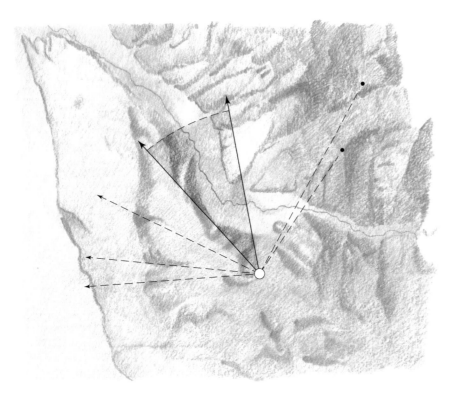

(*Above*) Woody Creek Garden commands a strong presence over its high-mountain setting. The structured garden is oriented toward the north and aligned to the valley below. In the distance, mountain peaks punctuate the horizon.

(*Right*) Water spills over a rim of honed black granite, fracturing on a rough stone wall before falling into a narrow channel below.

(*Following pages*) The pool, a thin sheet of water over granite, captures the form and silence of the hovering aspen forest and the clouds moving overhead.

In the main entertainment space, the reflecting pool's infinity edge draws the eye toward the landscape beyond. A sculpture by Italian artist Bruno Romeda captures a view, creating a threshold to the far horizon.

(Above) Granite slabs provide a flat surface for sitting and add horizontal and vertical interest within the courtyard.

(Opposite) Throughout the property are found design details that enhance the experience of the landscape and views, such as a log storage area for the fireplace at the promontory overlook.

(*Above*) The house disappears into the north-facing forested hillside. Open meadows below the house were revegetated with native wildflowers and grass.

(*Following pages*) From the promontory, views to the north and west reveal the undulating topography of the surrounding mountains and valleys. Atmospheric changes are reflected in the patterns of changing light and shadow.

Outside the walled enclave, the landscape transitions back to the natural grade of the hillside. A sandstone path at the base of the outer wall leads to a fire pit overlooking the valley. Slabs of stone selected for their bench-like qualities encircle the fire pit.

TETON OVERLOOK

eton Overlook is a studied balance of wilderness and cultivation, and a garden where natural processes are encouraged. Natural edges form the boundaries, creating the experience of a designed landscape encompassed by nature.

Located on a north-facing slope, the home and landscape accommodate the hillside topography with elegant stone walls and level changes that offer privacy and protection from the elements. Simple terraces extend into the landscape, punctuated by carefully placed cottonwood and aspen trees, transitioning to borderless grassy plains that merge with the natural landscape.

Balancing the intimacy of shelter with the splendor of outlook

The Teton Overlook's sloping site north of Jackson, Wyoming, offers spectacular views of the Teton Range, including the Grand Teton, illuminated in the foreground by sinuous cottonwood bosques and ranchlands. The garden's sheltered space provides extensive outdoor living opportunities, despite the climate's challenges of bitterly cold winters, steady southwesterly winds, and significant shade. Achieving a subtle balance of protection and expansion in this dramatic and exposed location required special knowledge of seasonal changes, topography, and native plant patterns.

The landscape architect collaborated closely with the owner and the home's designer, Carney Architects in Jackson. The simple lines of the stone and timber home express its commitment to human utility and environmental sustainability. Natural materials and architectural details unite the linear series of living spaces that respond to the topography. The architectural style is grounded in a Western vernacular, with minimal impressionistic boundaries between the domestic and wild. In the tradition of Frank Lloyd Wright's Taliesin in Spring Green, Wisconsin, the design team employed the concepts of prospect and refuge in the interlaced interior and exterior spaces and in design that gives way to views of the valley. Exposure to the elements, a common concern in mountain environments, is balanced with protective devices such as a controlled entrance. The inspiration of Charles and Henry Greene's design for the Gamble House in Pasadena, California, is

A table for two sits under the protective cover of a pergola. The surrounding kitchen and cutting gardens offer color and fragrance in this intimate walled patio.

suggested in the use of natural materials such as stone and wood and the craftsman-like details of the courtyard pergola, walled gardens, and sheltered spaces.

The north side of the home, in contrast, offers generous outdoor spaces that are open to the Albert Bierstadt-like landscape of tall jagged peaks and a broad valley floor punctuated by stands of cottonwood trees. The house was rotated approximately twenty-five degrees from due north to capitalize on the site's expansive views and to capture the sun at the times of day when the owners would enjoy being outdoors. Natural topographic changes in the hillside have been accommodated by level changes and elegant sandstone walls that offer privacy and a respite from the elements. The terrace walls extend into the landscape, intersected by carefully placed and angled glacial rock deposits. These large chunks of Wyoming granite create topographic relief and establish a link to the native outcroppings found in the valley. Boundaries are blurred as the lawn blends almost imperceptibly into the native sage meadows at the periphery.

The entrance to the property meanders through an existing stand of aspen and spruce trees. The tree screen, which opens just enough to allow entrance to the property, buffers the persistent south-westerly wind, whose presence is a reminder of the extreme climate changes that can occur at any time in this high mountain valley. The auto courtyard, a square plaza with contrasting paving in a grid pattern, leads to the free-standing garage, dug into the hillside and sodded over with native grasses.

Two small sandstone columns mark the main walkway leading to the front door. An allée of tightly spaced native cottonwood trees flanks the entry walk. The linear character of this sequence is complemented on the west side by a series of garden rooms that are reflected in the windows of the main house, and by a wooden pergola overhead, both of which visually and physically connect the interior and exterior. On the east side of the walk, a series of walls and steps leads to the guest house, located uphill of the main house. Lush carpets of low-growing groundcovers, interrupted periodically by stone outcroppings, soften the edges of the walkway. Peonies and lupine bloom profusely in the microclimates created by the walls, and small gardens of herbs and cutting flowers lend an element of domesticity to this tranquil space. Trickling down high walls, the sound of water, an element not naturally found in this vast and windy landscape, echoes in the space.

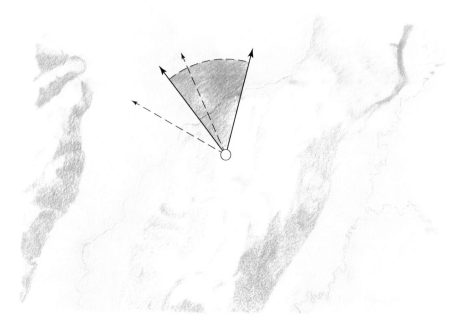

From its high perch above the expanse of flat glacial valley, Teton Overlook captures painterly views of the Teton Range, including the jagged peaks of the Grand Teton, Mt. Owen, and in the distance, Teewinot. In this mountain setting, the elements are magnified, and the garden offers welcome refuge.

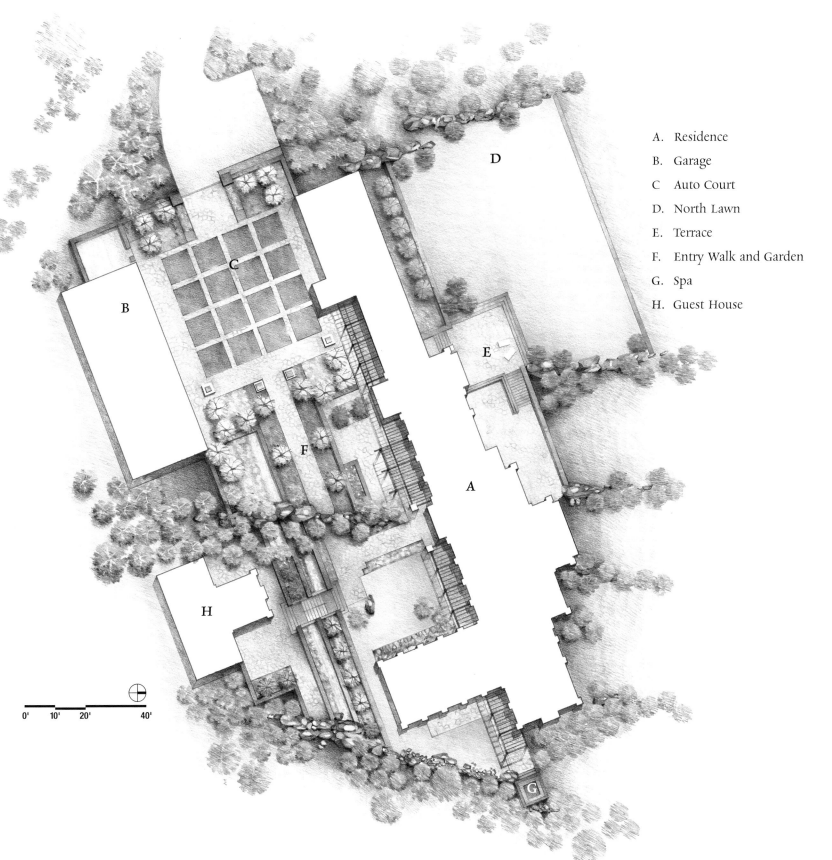

A. Residence

B. Garage

C Auto Court

D. North Lawn

E. Terrace

F. Entry Walk and Garden

G. Spa

H. Guest House

0' 10' 20'   40'

(*Left*) The driveway meanders through an existing stand of aspen and spruce trees and a rolling landscape. These elements were modified just enough to buffer the persistent southwesterly wind. The auto court views are contained by paving patterns, sandstone walls, and architectural features.

(Opposite) Separated by stone walls, planting beds brim with a variety of columbine (*Aquilegia* sp.). The soft blues and whites of these hardy perennials soften the walls and add color under a dense courtyard canopy of green leaves.

(*Left*) Lupines and daisies provide a colorful informal transition between the intimate domestic gardens located within the walled enclave and the existing native meadows.

(*Opposite*) A stone-edged spa is located next to the master bedroom. An opening in the aspen canopy reveals the Grand Teton in the distance.

(Above) Water spills over the lip of a granite trough into a basin. Iris (Iris *sp.*) and bellflower (*Campanula sp.*) add seasonal color to this intimate corner of the garden.

(Opposite) The lush microclimate of the south courtyard in midsummer transforms the entry walkway into a green tunnel of texture, light, and sound. Columnar and formally spaced native cottonwood trees stand guard over the walkway, which is bordered by carpets of creeping Charlie (*Glechoma hereracea*), lady's mantle (*Alchemilla mollis*), and other flowering perennials.

ASPEN TERRACE GARDEN

Complementing its formal architecture, Aspen Terrace Garden presents a series of open-air spaces that are transformed into intimate furnished outdoor rooms through elegant use of walled terraces, water features, and artistic lighting. The notion of landscape is explored as an extension of indoor space, allowing for graceful transitions for dining, entertainment, and relaxation.

Blurring the lines between indoor and outdoor living in house and garden

Finding a suitable location for Aspen Terrace Garden's home on this two-acre site overlooking the city of Aspen, Colorado, was a simple task for the design team. The challenges came with creating an extensive horticultural display on a north-facing slope in this high-altitude alpine environment, capturing and framing the city and mountain views, and designing large-scale outdoor entertainment and living rooms in context with the formal architectural style.

Located on a steep hillside amid groves of native Gambel oak, aspen, and spruce trees, the tiled-roof limestone home, designed in a classic style by Eric J. Smith Architect of New York, dominates its surroundings. To connect the stately home to its environment and provide a variety of opportunities for the owners to enjoy the setting and views, the design team created a series of terraces that physically and aesthetically support the structure. The views played an important role in the siting and design of the garden terraces. Parallel walls and elevated terraces modify the views and establish use areas and rooms, merging garden and architecture. The design team also focused on creating intimate outdoor spaces with warm lighting, comfortably elegant outdoor furniture, and a select palette of predominantly blue, purple, and pink perennials.

From the roadway above, a curved cobblestone entrance drive descends toward the home. It is rimmed by a series of stone retaining walls with crisp edges, stands of columnar aspen trees, and colorful

Anchored by a fireplace beneath a pergola, this outdoor room provides a comfortable and intimate scale for small groups and quiet conversation.

(Above) At the terrace edge, Peking cotoneaster (*Cotoneaster acutifolia*) hedges draw the line between the comforts of home and the valley beyond the precipice, providing the tranquility of a more controlled and domestic space.

(*Following page*) A transparent curtain of water spills over the lip of a semicircular fountain into a small pool below. The halo created by the veil of cascading water extends the transparency of light into the garden.

perennials. The drive enters the compound through an entry court. Opposite the front door, terraced walls define the outer limits of the property and accommodate the steep grade. Anchored by native shrubs and aspen trees, the terraces are planted with soft green and white groundcovers. A fluted and illuminated fountain, meant for viewing upon departure from the home, is set within the wall opposite the front door.

The garden, designed with traditional parterre patterns and geometric forms in mind, includes a series of small outdoor rooms that flow into one another. Lines and angles create vistas and visual interest, linking the house and garden spaces. Inside the home's various rooms, doors and windows draw in the natural views. Outside, the gathering spaces, water features, and planting beds are laid out in near-perfect proportion to one another, as extensions of the formal interior spaces.

The walls and terraces, which wrap around and buttress the home on the south, east, and west sides, creatively manage the steep slope, capture microclimates of sun and shade, and allow for a gracious flow of movement through the outdoor rooms. Architectural elements such as promenades and belvederes push the north-facing garden to the edge. Beyond the confines of the terraces, in the foreground, are homes and other structures consistent with urban development. Longer views of tree-covered slopes, ridgelines, and Basalt Mountain unfold in the distance across the Roaring Fork Valley.

Designed on several connecting levels, the east terraces intended for formal entertaining and dining capture and frame dramatic views of Aspen and the adjacent mountain valleys. On the lower level, tucked under a series of walls that extend the garden away from the house, is the more private grotto-like spa. On the middle level adjacent to the main living areas, a rectangular lawn with a fountain serves as the central organizing space and can accommodate a tent for large gatherings and events. Opposite the fountain and flanked by perennial beds is a dining pergola with a fireplace. Walls on the upper terrace enclose a large paved entertainment space that separates the garage and parking areas.

The west terrace, by contrast, is an intimate space outside the library, which is extended into the outdoors via a loggia. The terrace's high wall frames the distant views to the west, editing the neighboring development in the foreground. The space is anchored by a corner fountain in which a series of spouts extending from a narrow channel just below the top of the wall emit arcs of water into a pool. The white noise of cascading water is accentuated by the depth of the pool, creating a pleasing sound while masking urban noise for the terrace and the master bedroom above. Here as elsewhere in these terrace gardens, water is a constant element, offering a calming focus in an otherwise limitless landscape.

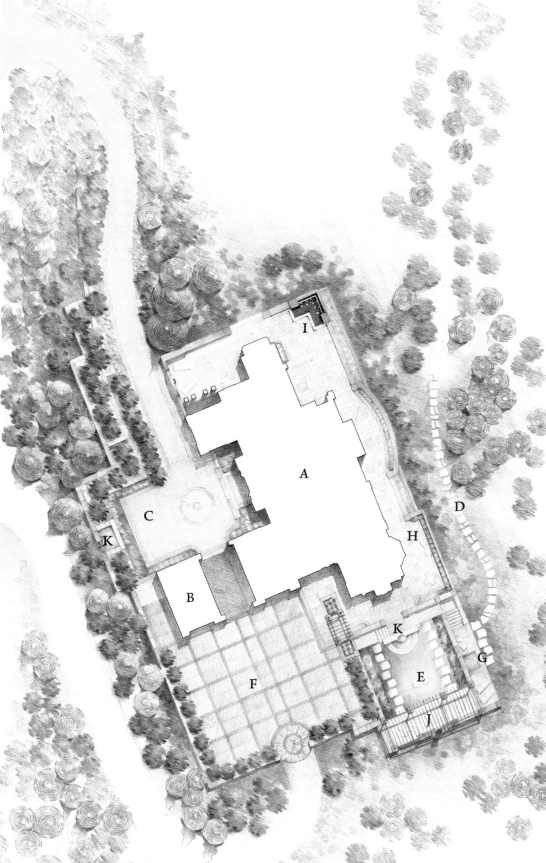

A. Residence

B. Garage

C Auto Court

D. Forest Walk

E. Entertaining and
   Gathering Lawn

F. Service Court

G. Spa

H. Elevated Terrace

I. Water Runnel

J. Pergola

K. Fountain

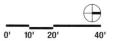

0' 10' 20'   40'

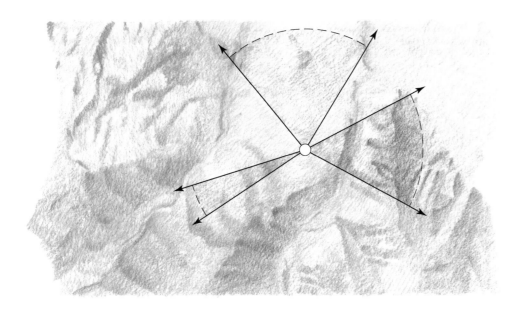

(*Above*) Set on a promontory high above the valley floor, Aspen Terrace Garden is embraced by a rugged landscape that provides sheltered intimacy. To the east, Shadow Mountain is magnified in the foreground. Long views to the north and west settle on the river gorge and glacially sculpted landscape.

(*Right*) An illuminated fountain set into a stone retaining wall establishes a warm and welcoming environment in the entry court.

ASPEN TERRACE GARDEN

(*Opposite*) From the arrival court, a custom pergola designed to echo the home's architectural details defines the entrance into the garden. Terracotta pots filled with white and green annuals and beds of lavender spilling over low walls welcome guests with color and fragrance.

(*Above*) The sound of falling water echoes throughout the garden. Fountains are an integral part of the landscape, providing focal points within the garden rooms and enhancing a sense of privacy that insulates the home from the sights and sounds of the town below.

(*Left*) Stone walls were constructed using a traditional method of mixing mortar with straw. Carved limestone caps and stepping stones intermix with the terraces. Seasonal plantings in garden beds include perennials such as delphinium (*Delphinium* sp.), peony (*Paeonia* sp.), purple salvia (*Salvia x sylvestris* 'May Night'), and an assortment of colorful annuals.

(*Opposite*) The driveway enters from a roadway above the home. Colorful perennials, including pinks (*Dianthus plumaris*) and Johnson's Blue geranium (*Geranium x* 'Johnson's Blue') and the annual blue lobelia, grow amid the white trunks of aspen trees and against the low limestone walls, forming a rich and layered approach to the residence.

CATALINA FOOTHILLS

Traditional cultural patterns and a rich visual display of native Sonoran Desert plants inform the structure and composition of this Catalina Foothills garden. A Modern design aesthetic combines color, texture, water, and shade to create an intimately scaled outdoor living environment, adding focus to a regional approach to landscape architecture.

Creating a comfortable outdoor living environment in the desert with color, water, and shade

Located on three acres in the Catalina Mountain foothills on the north side of Tucson, Arizona, Catalina Foothills has been highlighted in numerous local and national publications for its use of color, careful attention to the native plant palette, and greywater-reuse irrigation system.

The owners wanted to create a retreat for family and friends focused on the color, texture, and outdoor living environment of the desert Southwest. Inspiration for the home comes from the history and living environment of the region. The architecture by Suby Bowden + Associates in Santa Fe, New Mexico, takes its cue from the simple adobe structures awash in color found in Tucson's older neighborhoods, and other Spanish-Mexican colonial architecture. Color-washed walls with deep alcoves, intimately-scaled courtyards, clustered living spaces, and water and shade are concepts which, when combined with the architect's Modern aesthetic, result in a family compound that resembles a small village of houses cascading down a desert foothill. The landscape highlights the variety and richness of the many microclimates found in the Sonoran Desert. Contemporary art created by Southwestern artists is integrated into the home and landscape to capture the color, texture, and spirit of living in the desert.

Sandstone stepping stones allow for passage through the desert garden surrounding the pool area. A blue palo verde tree (*Parkinsonia floridum*) in bloom marks a stairway to the upper terrace.

A steep north-facing driveway leads to the home and garden. A gate laced with vertical strips of teak marks the entrance into the auto court. Another gate of painted iron opens into the entry courtyard. Stone walls and a heavy Mexican door distinguish the main entrance to the home. A trickle fountain, much like a desert seep, flows down a wall next to the gate, the sound of water reverberating in the small courtyard.

The home was designed to emulate a series of little houses, each with a slightly different color and character. The home is draped over a narrow finger hillside; twelve feet of vertical change exist between the main living area and the south ends of the guest and master suite buildings. The design team accommodated the grade change by designing outdoor spaces in a courtyard on two levels—the upper dining and entertainment terrace and the garden terrace and swimming pool below.

Four structures are arranged in a U-shape around the open bi-level courtyard, which faces south. The main living areas of the home are clustered around this central courtyard. A ramada in the northeast corner of the courtyard's upper level shelters an outdoor kitchen, fireplace, and entertainment area. A raised fountain, typical of those found in the courtyards of gracious Mexican homes, fills the space with the sound of splashing water. Colorful pots planted with agaves and cacti are placed strategically within the space. A retaining wall of fieldstone planted on top with red-flowering aloe separates the courtyard's upper and lower terraces.

A long north-south brick "street" connects the compound, stepping down from the enclosed sanctuary of the entry courtyard to the broad vistas of the lower courtyard's terrace and pool. Heritage oaks planted within this wide walkway recreate the historic pattern of street trees in the urban Southwest. The trees provide privacy, shade, and comfortable places to sit and relax next to the casitas, or guest suites. Lining the east side of the courtyard, the casitas are highlighted by walls and shutters painted in bright hues of purple, orange, and red. Across the courtyard, the master suite anchors the site's western edge. Characterized by rammed earthen walls and framed with sage green accents, the master suite opens onto the entertainment courtyard relatively unobtrusively.

The design team and owner worked creatively to achieve two design objectives that underscore the challenge of landscape architecture in a desert climate: capturing the color, texture, variety, and beauty of Sonoran Desert microclimates, and developing a waterwise strategy for the landscape by installing a greywater-reuse irrigation system. Tucson receives only twelve inches of rain annually, and is one of the nation's largest cities that depends entirely on pumped ground water. The future of this water supply is speculative, and the practice of applying water to the landscape could become a thing of the past. Arizona had just become one of the first states to create a greywater-reuse ordinance when the home and garden were being designed, and the team welcomed the opportunity to provide a model for the first residential greywater-reuse irrigation system in the Tucson area. Tied to all the non-septic plumbing fixtures, the pool filtration purge line, and all roof downspouts, this system, together with the use of native plants, is intended to reduce water consumption for landscape irrigation by forty percent.

Patterns of light and shadow offer a visual and physical relief to the color-washed walls throughout the day. Elegant ceramic pots adorn the brick "streets" that connect the clustered living spaces.

Desert microclimates are driven primarily by shade and water availability. All deserts offer a complexity of color, texture, and survival efficiency that, for a landscape architect, offer a mixed blessing of challenge and reward. Tucson is a natural arboreal desert, meaning that it supports a great variety of trees and shrubs. Catalina Foothills is located within an arid range of the greater Tucson desert that is characterized primarily by creosote bush and sustains winter temperatures below freezing. While the site is next to the foothills, it is not close enough to receive the slight amount of extra water needed to create a richer landscape environment. The home's water-reuse system allows for accumulating just enough water to maintain a more diverse garden.

The landscape architect chose a palette of native plants whose colors and textures would offer an organic contrast to the architecture and whose bloom sequence would coincide with the period of time when the owners are in residence. All areas beyond the immediate perimeter of the structures are designed to mimic the existing desert conditions and mix of plant materials. Sonoran natives such as palo verde trees, brittle bush, and creosote bush follow the natural sequence from built environment to native desert at the exterior of the property. Closer in, the master and guest suites are screened with ocotillo, blue agave, and acacia trees, allowing for a glimpse of the variety of plant materials that exists in desert landscapes.

In the interior of the site are found plant themes that reference Spanish colonial landscapes from missions and church yards of northern Mexico and southern Arizona. Evergreen shade trees are a common feature in streets and plazas, providing cool places for people in the heat of the day. Three ironwood trees, a hallmark Tucson tree, stand silhouetted in formation on the upper terrace. These native trees provide shade and cover for the placita, or dining patio, while the plantings on top of the walls reference another Spanish colonial pattern.

The full range of Sonoran Desert plant material is revealed in the pool area. The colors and textures that so distinctly characterize the desert cover the space, providing a constantly changing seasonal display.

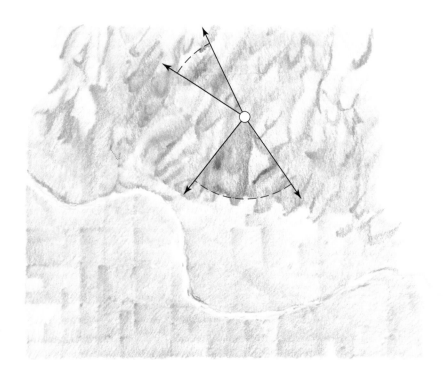

This Santa Catalina foothills home and garden, located on two lots on a promontory above downtown Tucson, enjoys views extending from the flat and rolling eastern horizon to the low hills on the western skyline. At the center of the compound, the courtyard pool and garden offer a calming sanctuary that aligns imperceptibly with the southern horizon and is suffused at dusk with the rosy hues of the panoramic sky.

A. Residence

B. Swimming Pool

C. Auto Court

D. Pool Patio

E. Entry

F. Ramada

G. Perennial Garden

H. Trickle Fountain

I. Interior Walk

0'   10'   20'   40'

(*Opposite*) A tile-mosaic mural draws the eye to the water's edge on the pool's east wall.

(*Right*) The angles and vivid wall color of the master suite's south wing contrast with the softer and more organic colors, shapes, and textures of the lower terrace garden. Throughout the compound, a palette of native plants integrates the architecture with the surrounding desert landscape. In this corner of the garden, a blooming blue palo verde tree (*Parkinsonia floridum*) announces the entrance to the master suite. Abutting the edge of the patio, barrel cactus (*Ferocactus cylindraceus*), pink New Mexico primrose (*Oenothera berlandieri*), and yellow bird of paradise (*Caesalpinia gilliesii*) are intermixed with native granite boulders to create a burst of spring color.

(*Above*) As evening descends upon the desert, subtle lighting appears in the garden and patio area. Along the east wall above the pool, a tile mural designed and installed by Santa Fe artist Sam Leyba comes alive with small lights embedded in mortar joints representing the constellations. The mural depicts the Aztec god Quetzalcoatl, the feathered serpent.

(*Opposite*) The bright blooms of desert perennials, including blackfoot daisy (*Melampodium leucanthum*), Angelita daisy (*Hymenoxys acaulis*), yellow sundrops (*Calylophus hartwegii*), and sandpaper verbena (*Verbena rigida*) provide a vibrant foreground to the pool and tile-mosaic mural.

(*Opposite*) An element seen in Spanish colonial buildings is repeated here in narrow walltop planters that display agave and red-flowering aloe (*Aloe* sp.) at the edge of the upper terrace and pool surround.

(*Right*) A fieldstone wall separates the "street" and guest quarters from the pool area. Aloes provide an attractive deterrent to walking or reaching over the wall.

(*Left*) The home was designed to emulate a series of small houses arranged in a U-shape surrounding an open bi-level and south-facing courtyard. A long corridor or "street" connects the compound, leading from the enclosed entry courtyard, past the guest suites, and down to the garden and pool terrace. "Street trees" in the form of heritage oaks (*Quercus macdanielli*) line the walkway.

(*Opposite*) The placita, with its lanterns, climbing roses, and colorful Mexican-style décor, is the focal point of the upper terrace. Three large native ironwood, a hallmark tree of Tucson and the Sonoran Desert, provide shade and cover. A trickle of water emanates from the fountain in the center of the space.

RIVERSIDE RANCH

Riverside Ranch, once a neglected landscape that had been a working ranch and then a road stone manufacturing plant, is now a picturesque fisherman's paradise. Imagination, commitment to preserving remnants of the valley's social and agricultural heritage, and a desire to recreate the landscape utilizing its natural systems prompted the restoration of the ranch and its transformation into a thriving new place.

Restoring a neglected ranch as a lush stream valley landscape

Riverside Ranch is located on a flat glacial terrace above the Roaring Fork River near Woody Creek, Colorado. The site appears to be a carefully preserved compound of historic buildings, set amid rolling meadows with long views to the surrounding mountain peaks and ridgelines. Forested glades, several ponds, and a stream replete with trout render a painterly impression of a thriving natural landscape. Behind this bucolic ideal lies the story of how creative design and much effort restored this badly damaged ranchland.

Until the 1980s, the site was part of a larger property that was home to a working cattle and sheep operation. At that time, construction on the adjacent state highway required the creation on the property of an asphalt batch plant to produce roadbed material. The site was purchased by the current owners in the mid-1990s, by which time the smaller sixty-acre parcel had become overgrown with weeds, and the ground was hard-packed, impenetrable, and strewn with piles of river rock. Multiple historic outbuildings, moved here by generations of ranching families, were scattered about the property. The owners wished to integrate the outbuildings into a more focused site plan and restore the buildings and landscape to the beauty and purpose of an earlier era, when the property and its cabins played an important role in the ranching and social history of the Roaring Fork Valley.

A stream, constructed to emulate high mountain riparian habitats, meanders through the property. Willows, cattails, and other aquatic plants are interspersed with boulders and smaller rock outcroppings, creating fish habitat in the shadows of the overhanging vegetation.

A once-neglected ranch house was rehabilitated, creating
a focus for the compound of historic buildings on the site.
Burning bush (*Euonymous alata*), Wood's rose (*Rosa woodsii*)
and other native shrubs are used as foundation plantings
around the house.

Lupines, daisies, and other native wildflowers create a transitional landscape between the manicured lawn area and the riparian meadows. The historic buildings are flanked on all sides by the great lawn, a vast entertainment space that pays homage to the era when this site was used for community gatherings.

The recreated ranch compound consists of the main ranch house, located below a bluff on the banks of the Roaring Fork River, and five historic outbuildings that were carefully moved, rotated, and, board by board, reconstructed in a domestic quadrangle that nestles against the steep bluff wall. The buildings, restored with designs by H3 Architects in Aspen, sit in a plane of native grass. The cabins' simple forms and dark-stained clapboard are roofed in corrugated metal, their front doors a bright red to match the restored main house.

The arrangement of shrubs and trees next to each cabin and within the larger compound is reminiscent of historic ranches throughout the Western United States. The main house and cabins are connected by a great lawn, an entertainment space that recalls an era when the property was used for community gatherings. Red-twig dogwoods, wild roses, and burning bush mark the front entry to each cabin. Groupings of cottonwood and poplar trees serve as focal points in the quadrangle. A meadow of lupines, daisies, and tall native grasses creates a transition between the lawn around the cabins and the riparian meadows. A shelter belt of spruce, cottonwood, and aspen trees provides protection from the prevailing winds on the west side of the property.

Despite the property's degraded condition at the time of its purchase by the current owners, it had plentiful water rights. An easement had been placed on the property dictating that it serve as a holding facility for water rights for all users and landholders in the immediate vicinity, so water storage was a significant factor in the site

design. To create a natural functioning riparian habitat for the stream, the storage areas were consolidated into ponds and integrated into the design. Material from the pond excavations was used to sculpt the flat site into more interesting topography.

A stream, constructed to emulate high-mountain trout habitat, meanders through the property. The trout habitat was enhanced by the placement of gravel spawning areas in the stream bed. Willows, cattails, sedges, and other water-loving plants grow along its banks. There are no formal path systems along the stream, though tree groupings, shrub massings, and rocks are placed strategically with fishing and exploration in mind. An occasional log or large boulder presents opportunities for fishing, stream crossings, or wading. The stream's water quality is monitored, as are the wetlands and stream flows from adjacent properties. Groupings of willows, red-twig dogwoods, and spruce trees are planted strategically to cast shadows and cool the shallow water.

The landscape offers a sense of respite from the busy highway that borders the property. Tall evergreens mixed with groves of cottonwoods provide a vertical mass that acts as a barrier and screen to buffer the sounds and sights of the highway. The ponds and the stream, which run continuously throughout the year, reflect seasonal changes, providing an interesting and ever-changing habitat for the natural environment that exists below the surface and along the banks. Tall grasses in the meadows tilt and curve with the topography, sway with the wind, and offer glimpses of the streams, ponds, and the horizon down the valley.

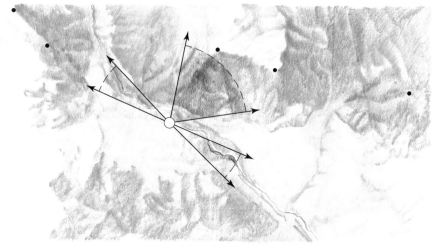

(*Above*) Set on a flat glacial terrace above the Roaring Fork River, the long and narrow property parallels the meandering river below. High ridges laden with pinon pine and juniper loom over the riparian landscape, directing views to the Continental Divide and surrounding peaks of the upper valley.

(*Left*) Architectural inspiration was drawn from the historic ranches of the American West, which turned to the land for their building materials.

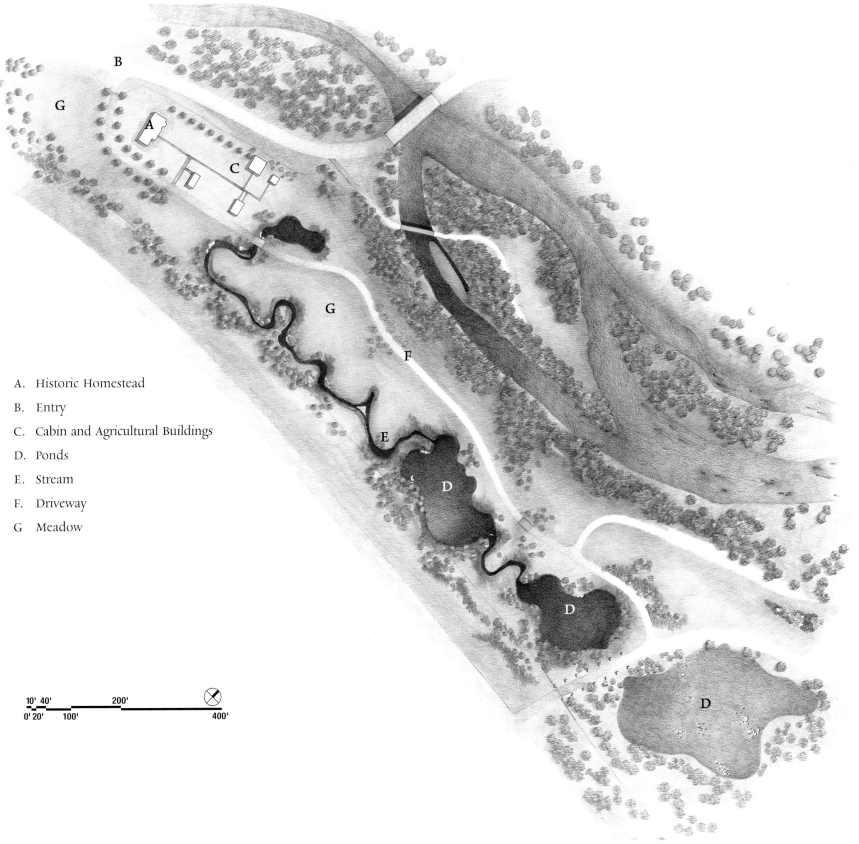

A. Historic Homestead

B. Entry

C. Cabin and Agricultural Buildings

D. Ponds

E. Stream

F. Driveway

G Meadow

10' 40'   200'   ⊗
0' 20'   100'   400'

RIVERSIDE RANCH

(*Above*) A modest wooden bridge in a landscape of red-twig dogwoods, cattails, and spruce trees allows for viewing the stream from above.

(*Opposite*) Groupings of willow (*Salix* sp.), red-twig dogwood (*Cornus sericea*) and Colorado blue spruce (*Picea pungens*) are planted strategically to cast shadows on the shallow water. Occasional logs and large boulders present opportunities for stream crossings, wading, and fishing.

(*Opposite*) Red-twig dogwoods offer a contrast in texture and color to the snow blanketing a stream during the winter months.

(*Right*) Pools reflect the surrounding landscape of wetland plants, meadows, and trees.

RED BUTTE GARDEN

At Red Butte Garden, simple shapes form relationships in a complex natural landscape defined by bold landforms and natural promontories. A perennial parterre garden and an elliptical pool are joined by a linear path, while a lawn terrace rimmed by a stone seating wall wraps around an Arts and Crafts house to display a sculpture collection.

The design of the perennial cutting gardens in the guest compound complement the Arts and Crafts character of the architecture, establishing a context for creating a colorful and fragrant perennial garden with a variety of bloom times presented by the mass plantings of daylilies (*Hemerocallis* sp.), yarrow (*Achillia millefolium*), astilbe (*Astilbe* sp.), Cranesbill geranium (*Geranium* sp.), and lupines (*Lupinus* sp.).

Defining a landscape using simple shapes and sculptural elements

At Red Butte Garden, the rural openness of the property is underscored by the sweeping approach of the landscape architecture. Simple bold landforms create natural boundaries throughout the site. Promontories and hand-crafted stone walls help to define the edges between the natural and the manicured landscape areas, which provide an outdoor exhibition hall for the owners' art collection.

Located next to the Roaring Fork River near Aspen, Colorado, the original four-hundred-acre Red Butte Ranch was developed by Chicago businessman Henry Stein after World War II. On a ski trip to Aspen in 1946, Stein purchased the property on a whim. He took advantage of its extensive water rights, developing the first gravity-flow irrigation system in the region to irrigate fields of alfalfa and grass hay on the property. Many years later, portions of the landscape remain agrarian, with a riding arena and equestrian facilities, as well as a tennis court and main house with wide valley views. The new owners' focus was to design and build a guest house with perennial gardens and a landscape in which to showcase their extensive sculpture collection.

The guest house and grounds around it were constructed on the site of the original ranch compound. In the redesign of this area, the design team was inclined to push the guest house to the edge of the rim overlooking the river to capture more of the river view. Doing this, however, would have eliminated the mature stands of cottonwood and

An extensive sculpture collection is integrated throughout the landscape, offering an imaginative and thoughtful perspective to the lawn terrace and gardens.

A curved wood bench provides a generous
platform for relaxing next to the pool.

aspen trees that offer protection from the wind and weather, providing privacy in an otherwise open landscape. Siting the guest house on the edge of the property meant that the entry and garden area would be located on the north side, creating a cold and shady environment and changing entirely the relationship between the house, garden, and surrounding landscape. The eventual solution—placing the guest house at the base of Red Butte—allowed for the structure to serve as a retaining wall for the slope above and for a larger lawn area to display artwork. The design placed the garden in the immediate foreground to the one-hundred-and-eighty-degree views of the river valley and mountains on the horizon.

The driveway enters the property through wooden ranch gates. Sloping gently to the south, it skirts the base of Red Butte, a rocky outcropping that marks the edge of the property. At a fork in the road, a line of mature native cottonwood trees leads toward the guest house; in the other direction lies the main residence. An irrigation ditch flows next to the driveway.

The design of the grounds within the guest compound is reminiscent of a classic Edwardian landscape. The owners' desire for a colorful and accessible cutting garden and the Arts and Crafts-style shingled architecture, by Shope Reno Wharton Architecture in South Norwalk, Connecticut, inspired the creation of lush and fragrant perennial gardens with flowers blooming across several seasons. Large masses of daylilies, yarrow, astilbe, Cranesbill geraniums, and lupines planted in a grid-like parterre create a garden setting worthy of an Impressionist painting. A linear stone path traverses the front of the perennial garden and terminates at a promontory overlooking the river. The path separates the home's geometric planting areas from the open expanse of lawn terrace.

Native Gambel oaks, which typically grow in masses, are trimmed and sculpted to frame views and create structural islands of vertical greenery in the middle of the lawn terrace. While organic and picturesque in nature, the lawn is a highly organized space designed to highlight the sculpture. Placed in the open or near large native boulders and clusters of oak, the stone and bronze sculptures are visually accessible but spatially distinct from one another and the larger landscape. A stone seating wall follows the contour of the land above the river, providing a finished edge to the lawn terrace. The seating wall offers places from which to enjoy views of the art, architecture, and gardens, as well as the river valley.

An oval pool, an existing element in the landscape, was adapted to fit the design of the guest house landscape. Tucked away from the more public areas, the pool and its surrounding sandstone terrace and outdoor grill pavilion define the southeastern end of the designed landscape. The pool reflects the green and gold leaves of a stand of aspen at the base of the butte, its rocky incline covered in evergreens. A wide curved bench frames the south edge of the pool terrace, offering a generous and quiet place from which to observe the changing seasons.

The guest house is linked to the rest of the property by a gravel trail that traverses the river's edge. When the trail emerges at the guest house from a sheltered canopy of trees, the landscape changes and the views open up, revealing semi-arid fields of grass and distant peaks. In the outlying sage meadow, the main house, perched on the edge of a bluff, stands in relief in an all-encompassing vista.

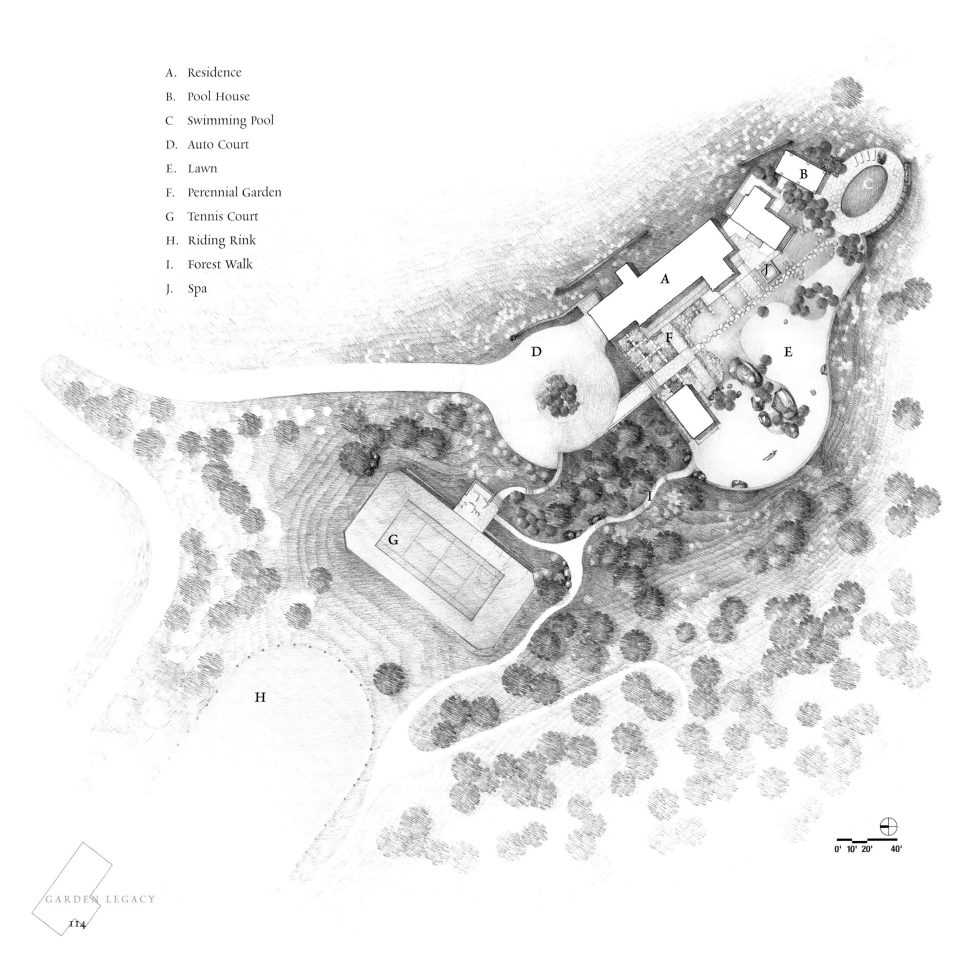

A. Residence

B. Pool House

C. Swimming Pool

D. Auto Court

E. Lawn

F. Perennial Garden

G Tennis Court

H. Riding Rink

I. Forest Walk

J. Spa

GARDEN LEGACY

114

0' 10' 20'   40'

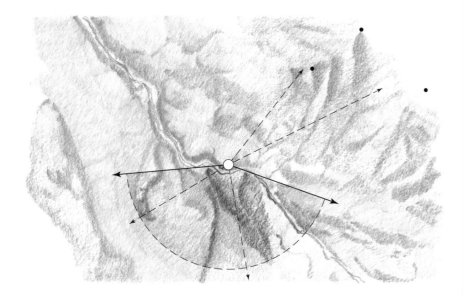

(Above) Red Butte, an imposing rust-colored geologic formation, is the setting for the home and garden which rest at its base on a glacial terrace overlooking the Roaring Fork River gorge. Above the flat valley and pasturelands, panoramic views to the south and west encompass high peaks and mountain ranges.

(Right) A boulder from the site and a stand of aspen trees frame the view of Red Butte to the east, defining the edge of the designed landscape.

(*Opposite*) An informal lawn terrace replete with existing stands of sculpted native Gambel oak (*Quercus gambelii*) provides exhibition space for the owners' sculpture collection.

(*Above*) Winter snow drifts gently over a hand-hewn sandstone seating wall. The brilliant crimson stems of red-twig dogwood (*Cornus sericea*) provide colorful vertical relief in a field of white.

(*Opposite*) Yarrow (*Achillea millefolium*) and daylilies (*Hemerocallis sp.*) bloom in early summer, followed by other colorful perennials, forming a rich impressionistic massing in the parterre garden in front of the guest house. Virginia creeper (*Parthenocissus quinquefolia*) climbs the decorative rain chain, offering a shade canopy for the porch in summer.

(*Right*) From atop Red Butte, the ranch unfolds to the northwest. The oval pool and parterre garden are nestled at the base of the butte near the guest house, with the lawn terrace arcing out to the edge of the slope overlooking the river. Other elements of the property include a tennis court, riding arena and equestrian facilities, pond, and agricultural meadows in the distance.

RED BUTTE GARDEN

CAPITOL VALLEY RANCH

The design for Capitol Valley Ranch conveys a sense of human comfort and scale in an expansive natural environment. In this rural valley setting, the architecture and landscape architecture merge to create a seamless transition between the built and natural environments. The generous use of glass allows for abundant natural light and encourages close relationships between interior rooms and outdoor spaces, joining the domestic and the wild.

Erasing the lines between indoors and out

Located on a bench of land overlooking the Capitol Creek Valley in Colorado, Capitol Valley Ranch is set low in the landscape, assuming an equal status with the adjacent ranch land, and capturing the panoramic views that surround it. The owners of this property, ranching and open lands enthusiasts, felt strongly that the home should not impose itself on the surrounding environment, but rather emerge from it in an organic and respectful manner. The agricultural and domestic areas are so successfully integrated that the wooden rail fences, visual markers in the landscape, are necessary only for keeping the horses and cattle out of the garden areas.

Designed by Cottle Carr Yaw (CCY) Architects Ltd. in Basalt, Colorado, the home was inspired by the designs of Cliff May, the 20th century architect credited with recreating the modern American ranch house. The home combines Western ranch house style with an element of modernism. The long central form and wings that extend out into the landscape invite nature to become as much a part of the home as the furnishings. Arizona sandstone is used indoors and out for floors and patios. The indoor and outdoor spaces are separated only by windows, doors, and walls, with no changes in levels between interior and exterior spaces.

Masked by subtle berming and tree massing, the house is virtually invisible from the ranch road leading to the property. A grouping of ponderosa pine and cottonwood trees and a simple loafing shed for the horses mark a turn in the driveway, indicating the north-facing

(*Above*) Native grasses edge the lawn and water, providing a fine-textured foreground for the long views of the mountains.

(*Opposite*) The living room terrace transitions to a lawn area that stretches to the pond.

entrance to the ranch house. The square graveled entry courtyard is enclosed by hand-hewn stone walls and softened with native shrubs and colorful perennials. The agricultural landscape beyond appears through openings in the walls, enhancing the sense of being a part of the larger landscape. The entrance to the home is announced by a brilliant persimmon-colored front door, flanked by an amur maple and garden beds of hosta, Rocky Mountain columbine, and blue Cranesbill geranium.

Like most agricultural lands in this valley, the property relies upon water provided by the seasonally flowing irrigation ditches that crisscross the surrounding ranches. One of three ditches running through the property is diverted into a small pond on the south side of the house. Trees and wetland shrubs planted around the pond help to frame the foreground in the long views to the mountains. The ditch, emerging from the other side of the pond and rerouted around the house, is planted with cottonwood trees, masses of willows, and red-twig dogwoods to recreate the natural plant patterns seen along ditches in the area.

The outdoor living areas close to the house provide a sense of protection and comfort, transitioning to the agrarian and native environments through the use of indigenous plants and water. The north courtyard, framed by a U-shaped section of the home's rock and wood walls, is open to the sky but protected from the elements. Away from the big view, the courtyard is focused on activities extending from the interior rooms, including the living room, which connects to the sandstone patio through large floor-to-ceiling glass walls and doors. Anchored by a rock fireplace and large rectangular seating boulders,

the patio is set tight against the home. As it merges into the garden area, the sandstone floor gradually fractures and becomes a soft carpet of creeping thyme and grass. An upright rectangular boulder serves as a point of reference, marking the transition between the seating area and the lawn. The perennial cutting garden is filled with flowers and herbs that bloom from spring through fall, including tall blue delphiniums, red and yellow yarrow, white daisies, and purple liatris. A simple post and wire fence marks the perimeter of the space.

On the sunny south side, the patio spans the entire side of the home, opening to the wide valley landscape. Floor-to-ceiling glass walls allow for transparency between indoor and outdoor spaces. A series of low rock walls running both perpendicular and parallel to the house help to define the outdoor living spaces. Sun-loving perennials bloom in walled garden beds adjacent to the kitchen and master bedroom doors. The sandstone patio is level with the interior rooms, extending twenty feet from the house to a lawn area meant for play and outdoor entertainment. Beyond the lawn, the pond and strategically placed groupings of aspen and spruce trees provide foreground and structure to the spacious landscape. A lap pool stretches perpendicularly from the house, with a spa set into the stone patio at the far end. Beyond the lawn and around the edges, tall native grasses, wetlands, and pasture lands spread out across the valley toward the mountains.

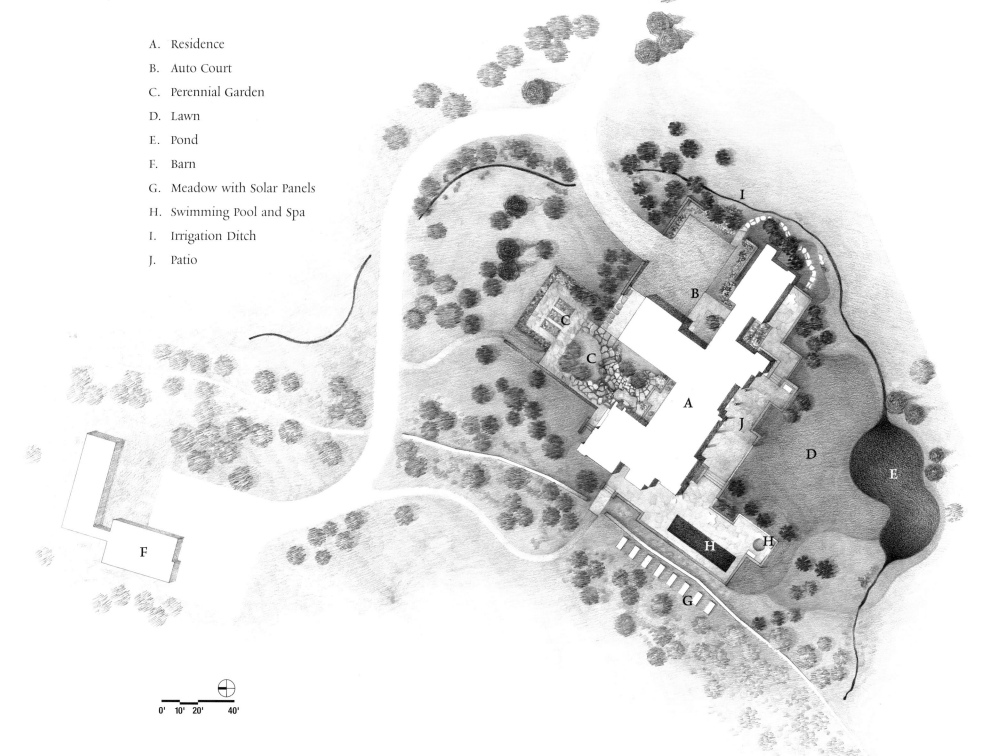

A. Residence

B. Auto Court

C. Perennial Garden

D. Lawn

E. Pond

F. Barn

G. Meadow with Solar Panels

H. Swimming Pool and Spa

I. Irrigation Ditch

J. Patio

0' 10' 20' 40'

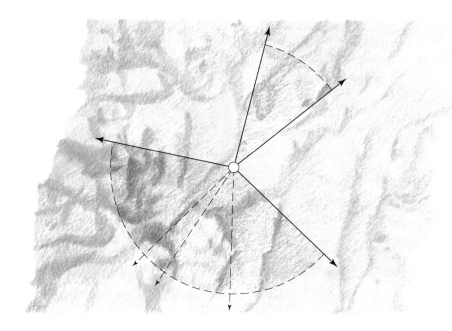

(Above) Agricultural meadows delineated by fences and irrigation ditches provide a soft and harmonious foreground to a wide valley bounded by treeless ridgelines and high peaks. This transitional landscape grounds Capitol Valley Ranch in its pastoral setting and seamlessly integrates the built and natural environments.

(Right) Creeping mother-of-thyme (Thymus serpyllum) softens the sandstone in the north courtyard. An upright boulder marks the point of transition from the patio to the lawn.

(*Above*) The north-facing entry courtyard is enclosed by stone walls, creating a private arrival experience that contrasts to the wide views and grand spaces on the south side of the home.

(*Opposite*) The cool blues of Johnson's Blue geranium (*Geranium 'Johnson's Blue'*) and Rocky Mountain columbine (*Aquilegia caerulea*) contrast with the vibrant persimmon-colored front door. An amur maple (*Acer ginnala*) adds a soft texture to the stone and wood façade of the house.

(*Above*) A fireplace and large granite stone benches anchor the sheltered north courtyard. Rocky Mountain columbine (*Aquilegia caerulea*), Jacob's ladder (*Polemonium caeruleum*), and delphinium add seasonal blue color.

(*Opposite*) On the north side of the house, an enclosed garden blooms profusely throughout the summer. Raised beds contain vegetables and herbs. The perennial cutting garden includes a seasonal selection of delphinium (*Delphinium x Pacific Giant*), purple salvia (*Salvia x sylvestris* 'May Night'), yarrow (*Achillea* 'Moonshine'), and bellflower (*Campanula persicifolia*).

(*Left*) On the sunny south side of the house, a lap pool extends into the landscape on a north-south axis. The dark bottom of the pool accentuates the reflective nature of the still water. Red window accents and patio furniture add lively color to the wide sandstone patio.

(*Opposite*) The protected north side of the home features a courtyard with seating area, a lawn, and perennial gardens viewed through glass walls.

(*Following pages*) The colors and textures of red-twig dogwood (*Cornus sericea*) and Wood's rose (*Rosa woodsii*), mixed with columnar groupings of aspen trees add distinct contrast in the winter fields of snow.

(*Above*) The mid-summer blooms of delphinium catch the morning light in the cutting garden.

(*Opposite*) Foreground views from the south side of the home are punctuated with stands of trees and wooden fences, breaking the expansive views of pasturelands and mountains in the distance.

DESIGN PRINCIPLES

Legacy gardens embody the expression of many carefully considered design principles. Each plays a role, such as creating atmosphere, defining space, or providing a focus for the garden. The following design principles offer insight into the concepts that guide Design Workshop's creation of legacy gardens.

Light and Shadow

The thoughtful placement of light in a garden allows for layering and contrast. In both small and large gardens, light and shadow have the ability to use transitory change as a design element throughout the day, season, and year.

The Garden at Night
Fine art, whether a painting or a garden, transforms in varying light conditions to reveal interesting details in composition. The contrast between a garden in full sunlight and a garden at night is exemplified by lighting. At night, a granite sculpture uplit from its base highlights the sculpture's interior texture, presenting an image that is completely different in daylight. A pool with a concealed light source produces a mysterious ambient light that reflects on the surface of the water.

Contrasts

The concentration of sunlight at high altitudes intensifies the contrasts between light and shadow and causes colors to appear more vivid. Contrast attracts the eye. Light and shadow alter perceptions of form, texture, and distance; bathed in light, a hard smooth surface such as stone paving may appear closer, while foliage in the shadows next to the paving appears to recede. Contrasts between light and dark colors and in form and texture create an interesting tension in the composition.

Changing Patterns

Light and shadow are integral to landscape architecture because they reveal textures and patterns on horizontal and vertical surfaces. Light—direct and bright or diffuse and soft—can reveal and distinguish dimensions on flat surfaces. Moving water reflects light, creating pockets of color, shadow, and movement in the surrounding surfaces.

Encountering the Land

The design for a garden can be enriched by using materials found on the site. Local flagstone used for paving or fieldstones used for building walls or as sculptural elements can provide a singular experience of place. Using native materials also grounds the landscape within its surrounding environment, creating a more seamless transition between the built and natural.

Paving

Paving materials form the horizontal surface—the ground pattern—of a garden and are an essential element for reinforcing and unifying the character of a space. In placement, color, shape, and craftsmanship, paving materials offer textural interest to the garden beyond that provided by the plants. More intimate garden spaces generally require smaller paving materials. Bands of paving in a different color or texture can be used for wayfinding in a large garden. They also add dimension to expansive horizontal planes, such as driveways and large patios.

Pervious Pavements

Paving that allows rain or irrigation water to percolate below the surface is important for plants and for maintaining healthy groundwater supplies. Pervious paving materials such as sand and gravel address this need by providing permeable horizontal surfaces. A hard surface such as a stone path can be "softened" by separating pieces of stone or other paving with grass or sand, which also allows water to be absorbed into the soil and creates an interesting transition from one space to another within the garden.

Sculptural Elements

Large native boulders can be used in a sculptural way to provide three-dimensional focal points that give a sense of permanence and illustrate the region's geologic history. Boulders can be used in numerous ways, such as marking a curve in a pathway and anchoring the end of a wall. Other natural features, such as groupings of trees or topographic changes in the landscape can provide sculptural interest. In a large garden or property, art sculpture offers scale and focus.

Material

Materials used in a landscape can be soft, such as earth, grass, vegetation, and water, or hard, including stone, wood, pavement, and gravel. The texture, quality, and durability of materials determine their appropriate use in the garden.

Style in Craftsmanship

The manner in which materials are crafted and joined can convey different garden styles. Refined materials with sharp edges and clean jointing suggest a more formal character and function for a garden space, while rustic or less uniformly crafted materials lend a tone of informality. Vertical surfaces are most successful when they accentuate the three-dimensional quality of the landscape. The addition of moss or lichen-covered rocks can add contrasting color and texture in a stone wall.

Sustainable Materials

Garden design becomes more sustainable with the use of materials from the region. Careful consideration of all available local materials should be given before looking elsewhere for exotic or non-native resources. In most cases, creative use of local materials, which are both less costly and do not require long-distance shipping, can render a landscape both artful and regionally attractive.

Movement and Direction

Directional movement in a landscape can follow the lay of the land or it can be visually and physically manipulated to achieve a particular design goal. Some of the most interesting gardens are those in which a pause is created by a device such as a narrow passageway or a large-scale vista. Others entice by suggesting the discovery of a "secret" garden or by the discrete placement of a special object in the landscape.

Movement and direction can be implied by establishing a line in the landscape with a row of trees, a path that disappears into the horizon, or an infinity-edged pool. Both the journey and the destination are part of this sense of movement and direction in the garden.

Order and Structure

A garden reflects the underlying patterns and forms of the surrounding landscape. Topography and the availability of water dictate land use, determining the order and structure of an intimate garden space or a larger landscape.

Pattern and Relationship

In every garden a distinct pattern and relationship exist between individual elements. A garden is more successful when those relationships are purposeful and ordered. Order can refer to the sequence in which an element or pattern is revealed or repeated, such as a focal point at the end of a long meadow, a series of stepping stones over water, or the repetitive and regimental use of trees as vertical elements in a horizontal paving sequence. A change in pattern can provide a visual clue that announces an entrance or a progressive change in scenery.

Horizon

Horizon, the point where the land becomes the sky, can be altered in a garden to change perspective and view. The horizon viewed from an open space is completely different than the same horizon viewed from a framed space like a window or door. A horizon can be established by shaping the land to elevate the point at which it meets the sky or by elongating a water feature. Elements can be edited from view so the garden space appears larger than it is.

Establishing a Line with the Sky

Some gardens are so intimate and introspective that the sky in proportion becomes an overhead dimension. In Western landscapes, however, the sky and the horizon line are integral to the order, structure, and *raison d'etre* of the place. Garden design offers numerous opportunities for integrating the place where the earth and sky come together. The appearance of this line can be intensified by changes in the view plane, level, or framing.

Framed View

In the American West, gardens and outdoor spaces often are oriented toward beautiful and truly spectacular views. A simple foreground and structured edge can intensify and enhance these views, occasionally changing the very perception of place. Trees, garden structures such as arbors or pergolas, and windows cut into walls can create picture frames, bringing into focus specific distant views. Details such as water runnels, three-dimensional objects, and even simple pattern adjustments at the garden's edge, can frame the views of the larger landscape.

Perspective

Creating perspective can change the look and feel of a garden quite dramatically. The horizon line can be altered to create a new perspective by using thoughtful design to edit out undesirable elements in the foreground. Subtle manipulations can improve a view or even generate a view where none existed. When elements in a garden are placed close together or close to a point of observation, for example, the garden edge and the spaces between appear larger than they really are, and the sky and the land merge to the point where they are equal.

Panorama and Distant View

Homes and gardens often are placed in the landscape to take advantage of a view to a distant peak, a body of water, or a valley below. However, such views can entirely overwhelm a domestic landscape if not managed appropriately. Introducing elements such as trees, sculpture, or water into the foreground of a landscape with endless vistas can help to adjust the size and perception of the view to a more comprehensible dimension.

Water

Water is a natural element in a garden. It anchors a garden site and can become a dominant feature by reflecting the surrounding environment in its surface and directing sound, motion, and light. Water nourishes plants, animals, and people, providing life-sustaining moisture and nutrients, adding sensual delight to a larger landscape. In the mountains of the American West, streams flowing over waterfalls and gathering periodically in ponds and pools suggest the natural forces of nature.

In desert climates, water is scarce and precious. Water is the most important feature in a desert garden, and its use is reserved for special purposes, such as providing a sense of coolness, refreshment, and serenity in an otherwise hot and arid environment. Where space is limited, a simple trickling fountain or small pool can provide the soothing sights and sounds of water.

Sound

From source to sea, water animates the landscape with movement in its quest to reach the lowest topographic point. The power of the sound water produces can vary widely, from unbridled and dramatic to controlled and peaceful.

Reflectivity

Water can act as a mirror, reflecting patterns on its own surface or from the sky and its surroundings in the garden. It also can create a sense of the ethereal, as in an infinity pool floating over the edge of a terrace or a reflecting pool capturing cloud patterns on the water's surface.

States

Water can change the character of the setting and create an interesting dynamic through its use in forms such as steam, ice, or a still mist. Moving water reflects light, creating pockets of color, shadow, and movement in the surrounding surfaces.

Focus and Punctuation

In every garden, there is a hierarchical structure and a layering of forms that point to that idea or vision that is of primary importance in the space. Spacial punctuation is manifest in many forms, including a change in materials, a unique sculpture, a group of evenly spaced trees, a plain of ornamental grass, a water feature, or a framed view. A focal point can be in the center of the view, occupying the space in a way that is meant to be seen. It can also be subtle and appear effortless, like a simple boulder in a field of wildflowers.

Space

Space is the definable environment of openness and enclosure. It can be the compression of a small garden room or the expansiveness of the large meadow. Space directs use in an inherent relationship between form and function. A space with a low ceiling, defined by walls, plant material, or natural topography, is intimate and calming. Space without enclosure seems boundless and imbued with kinetically oriented energy.

Enclosure

Enclosures of various kinds can define the quality and use of a space. Edges created by walls, hedges, fences, or plants create different experiences in the landscape. An overhead tree canopy can provide a transparent roof that gives structure to a space and defines the character of the enclosure.

Atmosphere

Gardens are affected by seasons and sun angles, humidity and aridity, and temperature fluctuations. With the changing seasons come intense changes in light and shadow. In full sun at noon on a midsummer's day, the colors and textures of a garden at the peak of its bloom may appear flat and faded. The same garden at dawn displays fresher, more vivid colors and textures. In midwinter, low and more indirect light intensifies shadows, showing greater contrasts in horizontal and vertical planes than appear during the summer months. At high altitudes, the lack of humidity coupled with the sun's intense rays produce color and contrast that cannot be duplicated at lower and more humid elevations. The presence of fog or steam can change an open and vibrant space into a moodier scene of shadows and anonymous features.

Planting Design for Legacy Gardens

Legacy gardens, like all gardens, communicate a personal design process. Some are artistic renderings, and others are horticultural experiments, intent upon creating a certain mix of seasonal colors and textures in the arrangement of plants. Some focus on a distinct space defined by garden walls, while others assume an important role in a much larger landscape. Many extraordinary gardens express cultural influences, such as regional garden styles or use of materials, or as a complement to architecture.

What ties these extraordinary gardens together and to their environments is a plant community that expresses a design idea while acknowledging the natural systems that encourage plants to flourish in their native environment. Gardens naturally respond to changes in weather and season, such as variations in temperature, humidity, and light. Gardens thrive as part of a relationship created by people, plants, and the place in which they live and grow. Treating plants and the natural environment as partners is the key to a garden's success.

Planting design is a process of visualization, imagination, and, most important, knowledge about the specific site, the surrounding natural environment and conditions, and the plant species. Environmental factors—wind, water, sun, shade, and soil—influence a planting design. The most successful planting designs use plants with an understanding of these factors and of the needs and character of individual species and their responses to climate and particular locations. In some cases, gardens are idealized versions of their surrounding environments. This is particularly evident in arid environments where a modest amount of additional water can turn a brown landscape into a verdant and blooming paradise.

As with all living things, plants rely on one another for survival. While the plants found in mountain and desert gardens differ significantly, their roles are similar. Groundcovers spread horizontally across a garden surface, insulating and protecting the moisture in the soil. Over-story elements, such as trees and tall shrubs, provide shade to cool hot summer days. Perennials grow quickly, producing colorful blooms, interesting forms, and foliage textures that when placed in particular groupings provide focal points within larger garden spaces. Gardens evolve as these living focal points change with the seasons and the cycles of life.

Plant Patterns

The most successful gardens replicate the communities and patterns of the native-plant community. Native plants are especially effective because they reinforce the inherent characteristics of the site—the horizontal and vertical patterns, bloom sequences, and seasonal changes that reflect the plants' ability to adapt to the soils, climate, wet or dry conditions, and intense sunlight, all of which are relevant to gardens in the West.

Landmark Plants

Plants often are the most dominant feature in a garden and provide a focus for the design. Used singly or in groupings, landmark plants, or plants that grow only in a particular region, can serve as a focus to represent the color, texture, and form of plants in that region. An example for gardens in the Sonoran Desert region is the tall ironwood tree with a spreading bluish-grey-green-leaved canopy.

Color, Texture, and Form

Gardens reveal nature's ability to produce plants that vary infinitely in color, texture, height, and form. Creative design considers how the characteristics of plants can be combined to create special places. Characteristics might be combined to create contrast, such as tall and short plants, spiky and mounded foliage, and colors from opposite sides of the color wheel, such as tangerine and lapis blue. The background against which plant communities are displayed is as important as the plants themselves. Wide swaths of a single color are most successful because they create a sense of visual clarity and harmony.

Plant Palette

The gardens represented in this book showcase plant material that is hardy and xeric, thriving in climates that are defined by short growing seasons and extreme temperature fluctuations.

Adequate winter moisture can transform the subtle earthen hues of a desert landscape into a vivid and painterly palette, suggesting however fleetingly, a lush environment.

In the mountains, short summers and concentrated high-altitude sunlight yield an unusually brief and brilliant perennial blooming season, producing floral combinations not typically found at lower altitudes where flowering times do not always overlap. As in desert gardens, microclimates in mountain gardens that are created by enclosed or protected spaces and an increase in water promote a proliferation of color and extend the bloom time. Similarly, a winter landscape suddenly becomes engaging with the addition of colorful and sculptural materials which add texture to an otherwise monochromatic scene.

The following pages provide a pictorial description of the range of plants that are available for mountain and desert gardens. Of paramount consideration for each landscape are the seasonal characteristics of the region. For more information on specific planting combinations, consult individual chapters within this book. To obtain additional information or imagery, refer to horticultural reference books.

ABOUT
THE FIRM

Design Workshop, named 2008 Firm of the Year by the American Society of Landscape Architects, is an internationally renowned landscape architecture, land planning, urban design, and strategic services firm. With offices in the Western United States, the firm provides a wide array of services—from private gardens to large-scale mixed-use communities to resort redevelopment—for public and private clients in North America and throughout the world. Forty years of collaborative processes have generated projects and ideas that have placed the firm at the forefront of the profession, seeking to engage our culture while improving our environment.

A design workshop is a collaborative process that fosters an open working environment in which everyone participates and they are encouraged to offer diverse opinions and an attitude of discovery. From the beginning, Design Workshop has used a comprehensive and holistic approach to design and planning that considers first and foremost the preservation of the natural environment. We also focus on safeguarding existing communities and fostering new ones, creating connections, and leading change. The method to the firm's approach: All work is done at a variety of scales to understand the broader context of the situation. This allows people involved in design and planning with various levels of interest and authority to cross the boundaries that typically separate them, and integrates technical disciplines that ordinarily operate in relative isolation from one another.

Design Workshop has been at the forefront of planning, design, and redevelopment for many of the world's best-known planning projects for communities, resorts, regions, and conservation efforts. The firm transcends the surfaces of projects to dig deeper into the traditional elements of the profession—art and the environment—and to consider them along with community and economics, significant aspects of landscape architecture that often go unacknowledged.

While large-scale projects account for much of the firm's current portfolio, residential garden design has always been a significant part of our work. We imbue these very personal garden projects with our values in different ways, though all share the binding philosophy of sustainability and balance. The gardens represented in this book are the result of our ability to foster connections between people and mix ideas in what partner Todd Johnson calls "the strongest creative and problem-solving force in civilization."

Garden Legacy is the second in a series of books about Western gardens. *New Gardens of the American West* considered the influence of the vast Western landscape on garden design, using examples of gardens in Santa Fe and Aspen. Continuing this theme, *Garden Legacy* seeks to encourage awareness and knowledge about successful garden design ideas through discussions about the importance of designing for the site, selecting appropriate materials and plants, and responding to the environment—the views, light, weather, and other conditions—to create extraordinary gardens.

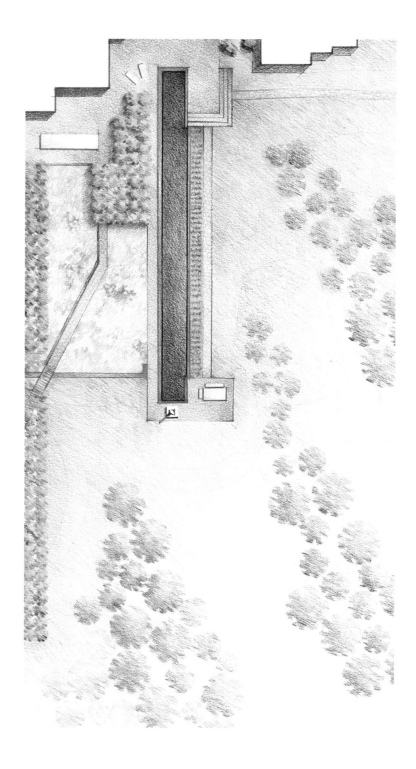

PROJECT CREDITS

Star Mesa Retreat

Principal in Charge:	Bruce Hazzard
Project Manager:	Deanna Weber
Landscape Architects:	Daisuke Yoshimura
	Amy Capron
	John Suarez
Architect:	Backen & Gillam Architects
Contractors:	Mineo and Associates
	Fine Homebuilders, Inc.

Snake River Residence

Principal in Charge:	Mark Hershberger
Project Manager:	Greg Stewart
Landscape Architect:	Bruce Greig
Architect:	William F. Tull
Contractor:	Bill Dziczyc Construction

Woody Creek Garden

Principal in Charge:	Richard Shaw
Project Manager:	Taber Sweet
Landscape Architects:	Jarrett Kest
	David Gregory
	Steven Spears
Architect:	Poss Architecture + Planning
Contractors:	Silich Construction and
	The Landscape Workshop, Inc.

Teton Overlook

Principal in Charge:	Mark Hershberger
Project Manager:	Greg Stewart
Landscape Architect:	Todd Majcher
Architect:	Carney Architects
Contractor:	Tennyson-Ankeny Construction

Aspen Terrace Garden

Principal in Charge:	Richard Shaw
Project Manager:	Kate Kennen
	Gyles Thornely
Landscape Architects:	Juan Lagarrigue
	Carolina Segura
	Mike Lusi
Architect:	Eric J. Smith Architects
Contractors:	Harriman Construction Inc. and
	Jim Robinson Land Improvements

Catalina Foothills

Principal in Charge:	Faith Okuma
Project Manager:	Claudia Meyer-Horn
Landscape Architects:	Sergio Yamada
	Wilbert Trujillo
Architect:	Suby Bowden + Associates
Contractor:	Willmeng Construction

RIVERSIDE RANCH

Principal in Charge:	Richard Shaw
Project Manager:	Valerie Alexander
	Taber Sweet
Landscape Architects:	Peter North
	Brian McNellis
	Gweneth Newman
Architect:	H3 Architects
Contractors:	B & H General Contractors, Inc.
	and The Landscape Workshop, Inc.

RED BUTTE GARDEN

Principal in Charge:	Kurt Culbertson
Project Manager:	Carolina Segura
Landscape Architects:	Robin Cheri
	Cameron Owen
	Maria Cagnina
	Chris Kiley
Architect:	Shope Reno Wharton Architecture
Contractors:	Shaw Construction and West Canyon
	Landscape & Irrigation, Inc.

CAPITOL VALLEY RANCH

Principal in Charge:	Richard Shaw
Project Manager:	Laura Miller
Landscape Architect:	David Gregory
Architect:	CCY Architects, Ltd.
Contractors:	New Age Homes and
	The Landscape Workshop, Inc.

Awards

Catalina Foothills

2010 Honor Award for Residential Design
American Society of Landscape Architects

Riverside Ranch

2010 Honor Award for Residential Design
American Society of Landscape Architects

Red Butte Garden

2009 Honor Award for Residential Design
Colorado Chapter of the
American Society of Landscape Architects

Woody Creek Garden

2007 Honor Award in Residential Design
American Society of Landscape Architects

Snake River Residence

2004 Sunset Western Gardens Design Award
Award of Excellence in Regional Category

2003 Merit Award
Colorado Chapter of the
American Society of Landscape Architects

ACKNOWLEDGMENTS

This book is the result of the steadfast partnerships Design Workshop has built with clients, in which every project pursues themes of discovery, trust, communication, collaboration, and refinement. We are grateful to the owners of these gardens and to the following individuals for their contribution to the design, development, and preparation of the book:

Richard W. Shaw, FASLA, whose design ideas are found in many of the gardens within this book, and who provided the foresight and leadership to guide this publication to fruition;

D.A. Horchner, whose photographic eye captures the essence of each garden not just as a piece of landscape architecture, but as a work of art;

Sarah Chase Shaw, whose knowledge of and love for gardens and the landscapes of the American West are embedded in the writing found throughout the book;

Lisa McGuire, Communication & Design, whose intuitive and creative graphic design skills made this book a work of art;

Kathleen McCormick, Fountainhead Communication, LLC, whose careful and comprehensive editing clarified the individual traits and larger purpose of the book;

Kotchakorn Voraakhom, whose graceful illustrative plans placed the gardens in their context and graphically communicated the nuances of their design; and

The members of the Design Workshop team

Project Management: Dori Johnson, Elyse Hottel

Prepress and Graphic Preparation: Nino Pero

Photography Preparation: Thomas Brunet

Base Plan Preparation: Ashley Allis, Mike Albert, Darla Callaway, Diedra Case, Julia Daruich, Brandon Hardison, Adrian Rocha, Carolina Segura, Steven Storheim, Kristen Walsh, Wayne Sanderson

Contributing Photographers:

Page 90, Kate Russell Photography

Page 128, Jason Jung/Estetico Group

FOOTNOTES

1. See Foreword to this publication, page 7.
2. Griswold, Mac and Eleanor Weller. *The Golden Age of American Gardens: Proud Owners, Private Estates 1890-1940.* New York: Harry N. Abrams, Inc., 1991, pp. 290-293.
3. For a complete breakdown of the Olmsted work in Colorado, see *The Master List of Design Projects of the Olmsted Firm, 1857-1979* edited by Lucy Lawliss, Caroline Loughlin and Lauren Meier. National Association for Olmsted Parks, Second Edition, 2008.
4. From 1925-1928 the Olmsted firm completed several subdivision commissions in Colorado Springs. The clients included Penrose, with whom the firm had consulted earlier regarding his estate.
5. Karson, Robin. *A Genius for Place: American Landscapes of the Country Place Era.* Amherst: University of Massachusetts Press, 2009, page 23.
6. Kelly, George W. *Rocky Mountain Horticulture is Different: How to Modify Our Climate to Fit the Plants and How to Select Plants to Fit Our Climate.* Denver, Colorado: The Green Thumb Council, 1951. In particular, see the preface to this second edition.

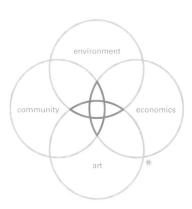

When environment, economics, art and community are combined
in harmony with the dictates of the land and needs of society,
magical places result. Places that lift the spirit. Sustainable places of
timeless beauty, enduring quality and untold value – for our clients,
for society and for the well being of our planet.